WERE YOU IN THE WAR GRANDPA?

W. J. Jackson

Namarrkun
Bristol

Were you in the War Grandpa
By
W. J. Jackson

A Namarrkun Publishing Company
Rock House, Bridgewater Road Bristol UK.

Copyright © 2017 W. J. Jackson. All rights reserved.

First edition published 2017 in the United Kingdom. A catalogue record for this book is available from the British Library.

ISBN 9780993285448 UK edition

No part of this book shall not, by way of trade or otherwise, be lent, resold, hired out or otherwise circulated, reproduced or transmitted in any form or by any means, electronic or mechanical, including photocopying, recording, or by any information retrieval system without written permission of the publisher.

Designed and Set by Namarrkun
www.namarrkun.com

Although every precaution has been taken in the preparation of this book, the publisher and author assume no responsibility for errors or omissions. Although information herein is based on the author's extensive experience and knowledge, it is not intended to substitute for the services of qualified professionals. Neither is any liability assumed for damages resulting from the use of this information contained herein.

Were You in the War Grandpa?

I dedicate this narrative to my Granddaughter Sinead, who asked me this question.

The discovery of my old diaries prompted me to write this insight of everyday life in wartime RAF. For me, life in the Armed Services was uneventful and cannot compare with the lives of those who suffered the horrors of active warfare, or became prisoners of war. It might, therefore, make boring reading, but it is strictly factual with no flights of fancy, with dates accurately presented.

723 JACKSON   January 2000

I am touched that such a question having come from my 10-year-old self, inspired you to share your story with us. The accounts of your travels around India during the Second World War planted a seed and have led me to want to discover the world for myself.

You are a lovely, modest, intelligent and dignified man who has made an incredible impact on my life!

Thank you, Grandpa, and Happy 90th Birthday!

With Much Love

Sinead Jackson   April 2014

Acknowledgements

I offer my wholehearted thanks to:

Jacquie Crowther and Richard Jackson for their hard work in bringing this text to fruition

Audrey Jackson for her scanning and editing skills

Bob Thornton for publishing this for me

JOINING UP

13th December 1943. RAF Cardington, Bedfordshire

Following the invasion of Italy, which had seen some of the hardest fighting yet, on the 25th July 1943 the Italian leader Benito Mussolini was arrested by his own Government. Although German Forces attempted to defend Italy, they were eventually driven out, the Allied troops being assisted by Italian partisan fighters. By the end of 1943, the war was going fairly well for Britain, and American troops were flooding in. Adolf Hitler, the German leader, had invaded Russia and his front line was slowly advancing towards Moscow. Stalin, the political and military ruler of the USSR, had asked the Allies to create a second front in Western Europe to ease the pressure on his front line. The British leader, Winston Churchill, was very wary as a previous invasion attempt in France had failed miserably, with a considerable loss of life. Stalin accused Churchill and the Western leaders of being afraid, but Churchill realised that his resources of troops and war machinery were not sufficient for an assault on the German Nazis who had full control in Europe.

Churchill therefore, consulted with Roosevelt, President of the USA and it was agreed that a second front could be opened with American troops playing a major part in the assault. A highly secret plan was drawn up to invade France in the region of Normandy, the assault troops leaving from the shores of Devonshire. The Americans concentrated in this region, and 25 miles of the south Devon coast at Slapton Sands were evacuated of all civilians. There the American soldiers learned assault tactics, with landing crafts discharging men and mobile weaponry on to the beaches, live ammunition being used.

This preparation meant full use of British soldiers, sailors and airmen. A sea-borne invasion needed full protection by the Royal Navy, and air cover to prevent bombing and strafing of Allied troops from the air. Conscription in Britain had provided a successful fighting force; with help from the British Commonwealth, we had been successful in North Africa, had won the air "Battle of Britain" and were now heavily engaged in the European countries. This put a strain on manpower in Britain, and women who had been doing sterling work in arms factories, were being more actively recruited to do men's work in farming, on the buses and in uniform in the ATS, WAAF and WRNS. Men who had previously been too young, or too old, to be called up were now being conscripted; but a new and urgent need had arisen - the mining of coal.

Conscription into the Armed Forces had left a serious shortage of miners in the coal mining industry and this was having a disastrous effect on the production of arms and war material. Ernest Bevin, the Minister of Supply decided that boys becoming old enough for national service could serve the Country equally well by becoming coal miners as becoming armed service men. Boys who took this option were henceforth known as 'Bevin Boys'.

I had my pre-call up medical in the autumn of 1943, and was told I could go either down the mines or into the Royal Navy. I was not too keen on either. Having gained a War Certificate 'A' in the OTC at school, and a War Certificate 'B' in the Senior Training Corps at Birmingham University, I was eligible for entry in the Army at OCTU level (i.e. pre-commission in the Infantry) or with an immediate commission in the Royal Marines. Of the four choices, I eventually opted for the Royal Navy, giving my reason as wanting to be trained in a technical trade, such as wireless telegraphy. My call-up papers arrived with instructions to join the RAF and proceed to RAF Cardington!

So on the 13th December, I left 61 Lichfield Road, Bloxwich at 6.30am on a cold foggy morning and made my way to the LMS railway station at Bloxwich with a rail warrant to Cardington, change at Birmingham and Bedford. As instructed, I carried an empty suitcase for the return of civilian clothes. A crowd of us piled out of the little railway station at Cardington and then began my introduction to communal life in the RAF. The huts were huge, containing 3-tier beds and there must have been 200-300 men in each hut, everybody bumping into everybody else. There followed a few days of intensive activity, getting uniforms and other kit, getting a number and marking every item of kit with that number.

I was given 3008723 and for the next four years I would be known as 723 Jackson; identification was always by your last three, initials didn't matter much. The stores ran out of "boots, rubber, knee" and I got a deficiency chit to confirm that I had no wellingtons (this will be mentioned again, later). In the barbers shop there were 10 or 15 chairs, barbers working round the clock to give everybody a short back and sides hair cut.

We were all given the lowest rank "Air Craftsman second class" (AC2 for short) and I was classed "Under training, wireless or radar mechanic". Everybody was given the lowest rate of pay (three shillings per day). Even though after the first or second day we all wore uniform, we were of course a shuffling straggling mob, but left in no doubt that this would very soon be changed. After the third day, a group of us waved goodbye to the big huts, the big hangars (where the R101 and other airships were made) and were put on a train to Skegness.

CALL - UP

War Office Certificate 'B' (Infantry)

WAR CERTIFICATE "B"

This is to Certify that

William James Jackson

a member of the Birmingham University
Senior Training Corps
passed the Examination for
War Certificate "B"

Infantry
R.E.
~~R.E.M.E.~~
~~R.A.M.C.~~

held on 2 & 3 April 19 43 at BIRMINGHAM
including the requisite Physical Efficiency Tests as
laid down in current War Office Instructions.

B.C.W. Johnson
Lt. Col.
Officer Commanding
Birmingham University S.T. Corps.

Countersigned.
The War Office,
London, S.W. 1.

R.N. Vaughan, Col.
Major-General,
Director of Military Training.

SQUARE BASHING

16th December 1943. RAF Skegness

"Skegness is so bracing", although I didn't know the slogan at the time. It was freezing, rather than bracing, when I arrived. The mob walked from the railway station, dragging kit bags and webbing equipment, and I was in a mob taken to Saxby Avenue and put in a detached house called Kathmarie. All the houses in the Avenue were completely bare, no lino or lamp shades, only some black-out screens for covering the windows during the evening. Iron beds were crammed so tightly in each room that there was hardly space to move. I was directed into a little upstairs room with two older bods, Hank Hemmings and little Flinty. Hank, was a Canadian of a mild disposition; he tried a few words of comfort when he could see by my face that I was less than charmed with the accommodation. He didn't finish the training course, as he was transferred to the Royal Canadian Air Force, for which he had originally volunteered. He had been living near Walsall, and he visited my mother in Bloxwich to let her know how I was coping. For training, we were arbitrarily put into Squads; I was put into No. 6 Squad with mainly older men and when I asked for a transfer to another Squad I was told "you're all in this together!" So during the time at Skeggy I was known as either 6 Squad or Kathmarie. In another upstairs room at Kathmarie were two bods who became firm friends, Fred Hill from Walsall and Bill Paling from Gloucester. Our paths were destined to meet and part several times during our RAF Service, and afterwards.

Every morning at 6.30am the houses in the Avenue would disgorge their occupants and in pitch darkness we formed one large crocodile, in three ranks. When the NCO at one end gave the order to march the men at the other end could hardly hear, so they shuffled along just following the one in front. Bods were all over the place when the road was icy. We had to carry our mugs in the left hand and swing the right arm. This meant that the bod on your left was always tending to knock the mug out of your hand. The roads were soon littered with broken mugs, mine included. This was annoying, because for the rest of the time in Skeggy I had to use my mess tin for getting tea, a flat metal thing, difficult to carry when full and awkward to drink from.

We marched down the Drummond Road to the Nottingham Boys Home, now converted to a cookhouse for feeding the erks (new recruits). The food was very unappetising, but fresh air and exercise soon gave rise to hunger. In fact, most of our spare time, which wasn't much, was spent looking for cakes and buns in various WVS canteens and tea bars (as in Woolworth's in the town centre). I think we went down to the Notts Boys three times a day. You washed your irons (knife, fork and spoon) in a bucket of greasy lukewarm water, most unhygienic. On kit inspections the NCO would hold your fork up to the light to see if there was any debris sticking between the prongs.

Training was done by the Squad, marching, arms drill and so on. The NCO in charge of no.6 Squad was very reasonable, named Cpl. Stubbs. He could tell that I knew as much about weapons as he did, but I kept dumb and he didn't show me up in any way. The PT instructor was a wiry little chap named Cpl. Weber. PT was done by the street, not by Squad, and as soon as we were dismissed into the billets by the Squad Corporals to change into PT Kit, he would run up and down the street shouting "C'mon, you should be out by now, lets-be 'avin you", to which we replied " no, we're Saxby Avenue."

Drill and PT were made very uncomfortable by stiffness in the arms after vaccinations and inoculations. Talks were given by officers in the local cinema. There were also films, and the one on contagious diseases caused a few bods to faint, and they were revived outside. We also had to do guard duties, assault courses, firing 0.303 rifles and sten guns, church parades and so on. Showers were excruciating; we had to undress and shower in freezing water in something like an old barn with no sides to it. There were 30 or 40 sprinklers, and you always ended up with wet socks and dirty towels. I was very lucky however, because a relation of my sister Margaret's husband, Evan, who lived in Skegness, let me have hot baths and sometimes a meal, although I tried not to take too much advantage of this (fuel and food were rationed, of course).

Christmas came and went so uneventfully that I don't remember much about it; we had the day off I think, and I went on my own to Chapel in the morning. One week-end early in the New Year Margaret came to see me. It was a good boost to morale seeing her, going walks together. I got some looks, an erk walking along with a smart young lady in high-heeled shoes! All in all, with boots and uniforms worn in, we felt pretty fit after two months of perpetual motion. Bods were posted off to many destinations and a small group of us were given rail warrants to London, for training as wireless or radar mechanics. I was pleased that Fred Hill and Bill Paling were in this group, especially Bill who was 10 years older than most of us and guided us on the Underground, and to somewhere where we had to find an RAF lorry which took us to Holloway Road.

RAF SKEGNESS

No. 6 Squad

BASIC RADIO COURSE

10th February 1944.   London, Northern Polytechnic

On arrival we were told the addresses of our billets. I went to a terrace, but very large, house in Highbury called the Cumberland, with a big green in front, and a factory (AC Cossor, an electrical manufacturer) behind. I shared a large upstairs room, with lino on the floor, with Bill Paling and four or five others. Compared to Kathmarie, it was spacious and pleasant. All meals were in the refectory at the Poly, although cocoa for supper was available in the basement of the house next door to the Cumberland.

We congregated next morning in the big hall at the Poly; we were told we were No.7 entry and were then divided into four classes. A lot of the bods had done their induction training at Arbroath, and most of these were billeted in Islington. Like the Squads in Skeggy, the classes split us up, but it meant that very soon we all got to know each other. Fred and Bill were in 7A, I was in 7C and Alan East from Sheffield was in 7D. Classes 7A and 7B had civilian instructors, 7C and 7D had RAF instructors, Corporals Jimmy Dubock and Chalky White respectively. The Officer in charge of the RAF at Northern Polytechnic was F/Lt Poyser, and F/Sgt Smith was i/c orderly room, "parades" and everything else. Chiefy Smith was a very congenial old boy, with goodness knows how many years of service. He took assembly every morning and one bod's name kept coming up - Exintravilonis. He would start off "Exit, Exiv, Extin…….. you know who I mean - that man!" Before the course finished that man had changed his name by deed poll to Nikitas.

Basic radio lectures went well, Jimmy Dubock being a good lecturer and tutor in the practicals. We had plenty of fun, but never chaos. A civilian instructor took us for metalwork, and various other people took us for First Aid, Aircraft Recognition, Engine Maintenance, PT, route marches and so on. We did Fire Watching in the Poly, for which we got paid 3s 6d and a free supper! PT and sports were held once a week in Finsbury or Tuffnel Parks; cross country five mile runs were round the streets, calling in shops on the way for buns and cakes. Once a week each class would "march" along Seven Sisters Road to Hornsey Road Baths where you could either swim or have a hot bath. The baths were in numbered cubicles, there being no taps, an attendant old boy outside the cubicles regulating the flow of water. A regular trick would be to call out "more cold in no.6" where the bod inside would be yelling "no, no, no more cold". The old boy would run up and down with his big key, grumbling. In one lecture room in the Poly there was piano and if an instructor was late arriving, AC2 Buckley would entertain us - he was excellent at boogie woogie. But of course, there were written tests every so often and every four or six weeks F/Lt Poyser would subject each one of us to a viva. Bods who didn't come up to scratch were posted off the course; one of these was a special pal of mine called Adrian (Taffy) Williams. We wrote to each other for a long time (his name crops up again later). Another bod was posted for stealing; nearly everybody kept in his locker a pot of jam for putting on bread and butter after the evening meal, and this bod took a jar out of somebody else's locker. I quite liked him, he was a mild mannered person and full of remorse for what he did and I was sorry he was sent down.

At first, bombing interrupted classes; when the air raid sirens went we had to get underneath our desks. This precaution was abandoned after a time as being too interruptive, the raids becoming more frequent and lasting longer. In the billets at night, there was similar action as bods became fed up with going down to the cellars. One night, (16th June) instead of the drone of the bombers engines we heard a different noise, which, when suddenly silenced, was followed by a big bang of high explosive. This was eerie and went on through the night. Next morning we learned that these were pilot less flying bombs, later to be known as V1 or buzz bombs or doodle-bugs. They came over by the score and eventually air raid warnings were scrapped because they were lasting 24 hours. Roof observers sometimes gave immediate local warning ("Imminent Danger"), and in the billets at night we only ran into the cellars when the Cossor factory imminent danger warning klaxon sounded (I think we soon got tired of this also).

One night when Chaddy Chadwick and I were firewatching at the Poly we were hit by a large H.E. bomb. We were on the second or third floor and later we judged it passed through the building within yards of where we were standing. Obviously, it didn't explode, or we would have been instantly killed. The whole building filled with thick dust, we could hardly see or breathe, the lights went out and we groped our way downstairs. In the main entrance, some ARP (Air Raid Precautions) men called us to get out. After hanging around in Holloway Road for some time, bomb disposal men came along and confirmed that it was an unexploded bomb, now buried deeply in the foundations of the building. Chaddy and I walked back to Highbury, observing on the way many houses demolished or burning. Next morning we were not allowed in the building and instead paraded in Tuffnel Park, from where we were sent home on leave with 5-day passes. The bomb fell on the 14th March and was removed on the 20th. We returned on the 21st March and lectures resumed, surrounded as we were with debris, with locker room (and jam!) destroyed, and windows out making it very draughty.

For one shilling a London Transport all-day ticket could be purchased. This covered the use of buses, trams and the Underground. Week-ends were always busy therefore, there being plenty of clubs to eat and lounge about in, such as the Welsh club, Canadian Club, Beaver Club, Nuffield Club, the Strand YMCA, Tottenham Court Road YMCA, and many more. There was a bureau in the West End where anyone in the Armed Forces could get free tickets for theatres, shows of all kinds, and dances. At Finsbury Park Empire I saw Geraldo and his orchestra with Doreen Villiers and Dorothy Carless, and Oscar Robin and his orchestra all of which were very popular at the time. I went to live broadcasts at the BBC; one I remember was Merry-go-round with Stinker Murdoch. I went to the Windmill Theatre to see Phyllis Dixey, to Madame Tussauds, Alexandra Palace Ice Rink, the Royal and the Palais in Edmonton, and so on. I remember going to several parties at a girl friend's house in Waltham Cross. It turned out to be a glorious summer, and with walks in Hyde Park, Waterlow Park, Tuffnel Park, Highbury Fields and Hampstead Heath, it was very easy to find girl friends. Names in my diary include Kathleen, Pat, Gwen, Winnie, Joyce, Sheila, Betty, Gladys, Sylvia, Marie, Eileen, Beryl and Lily. Lily worked at the Gaumont cinema in Seven Sisters road and every time we marched past there on the way to the baths, we would all shout her name and she'd give a wave if she was around. Sylvia worked in Woolworths and would always save a few razor blades for me, when they were available (standard 3-hole blades were very scarce). Sylvia and Beryl would sew buttons on for me, and darn my socks. There was never a dull moment.

Week-days were a bit quieter. Some evenings, Bill, Fred and I would walk into Highbury to the Continental Café, or to a Greek café for Wiener Schnitzel, or anywhere else for fish and chips; or finish off the evening in the basement of the house next to the Cumberland for cocoa. We would watch the searchlights and ack-ack guns, or play cards, or do a bit of revision if a written test or viva was coming up. On the 6th June we saw waves and waves of aircraft formations passing overhead. We did not know at the time that this was D-day for the invasion of France. It was only much later that we heard that the landings on the beaches of Normandy had been successful, with casualties lower than those sustained in practice at the end of 1943.

At the beginning of July we were told to leave the Cumberland and move to another billet in Highgate. I got a room with Fred Hill, Hassy

Hasler and George French (there were a lot of Georges in no.7 entry; George Walkiden, George Tickell, George Horrobin, George Lucas, to name a few). In no.7 we kept very much to ourselves, although of course, changes at the Poly were quite frequent (e.g. April 12th no.4 entry left, April 13th no.9 entry arrived, June 7th no.5 entry left, and so it went on).

Evening walks were mostly confined to Hampstead Heath. I had a look at the tombstone of Karl Marx in Highgate cemetery. A little more swotting was done as final exams approached. On the 31st July, class 7C had a party, which of course included Cpl. Jimmy Dubock, and a few friends from other classes, including Ken Kid, Mac Sadler and Fred Hill. We had been asked to state our preference for further training, namely wireless or radar. In general, those with the highest marks got into radar, but I believe nearly everybody got their wishes. All my closest friends got into radar. On the 1st August we were given 8-day passes and in high spirits went home on leave.

NORTHERN POYTECHNIC

Class 7C

GROUND RADAR COURSE

9th August 1944.   RAF Yatesbury, No.1 Radar Wing

Having left home at 6.40a.m. and standing on the train all the way to Bristol, then changing to get a local train to Calne in Wiltshire, I felt quite tired when I got to RAF Yatesbury about 5.0pm. It was a very large training camp, but most (or all) of the crowd from Northern Polytechnic got into one hut. We only lived there, our training was done at the Radar School, which was fenced off and had its own guards at the gate - it was a camp within a camp. It was a fairly long walk from hut to School and there was another walk in the evening if you wished to refer to your note-books; these were secret and had to be handed in at the end of every lecture, and signed out at the start. Practical sessions involved familiarisation with the, then, current types of ground radar, CHL (chain, home, low), GCI (essentially a mobile CHL) and UHF (ultra-high frequency). CH (chain, home) stations were still operational in the UK, but they could not detect low flying aircraft and their days were numbered. Overseas installations were designated COL (chain, overseas, low) and the UHF (being so small the sets were usually vehicle mounted and used for assault, or movement with an advancing front line) sets were called EW (early warning) or LW (light warning). Interestingly two widely used developments were hush-hush at the time, nylon and the magnetron. Nylon was mainly used in the co-axial cables (and still is) necessary for carrying high frequency currents. The magnetron was a "miniaturised" version of a highly secret development at the University of Birmingham, and allowed the use of frequencies so high that currents could not be carried by co-axial cables but had to be directed along rectangular-section tubes (like ducts) called wave guides. A slice of bread held at the outlet could be toasted in a very short time! We learned about the dangers of high voltages in the transmitters, a rotating time-base in the receivers, the rotating aerial arrays, electric supply generators (the ubiquitous Lister diesel engine), routine maintenance, fault finding etc. At night there was not much to do except visit the camp cinema, the NAAFI or WVS on-site canteen. On September 8th, the first V2 rocket fell on London. I was glad to be in Yatesbury, for the falling of a heavy H.E. device without any warning must have been terrifying.

The school was so intensively used that some weeks of the course were held on a night shift. One night, strolling down to the Radar School, Mac Sadler and I bumped into an elephant. We didn't know that a circus had been given permission to pitch its tents and animals within the domestic site perimeter; it gave us quite a surprise.

Travel from Yatesbury was limited to a radius of 20 (or was it 30?) miles, so at week-ends there was plenty of hitch-hiking to the neighbouring towns of Devizes, Swindon, Chippenham and Marlborough. There were plenty of lifts available from the Americans, whose vehicles sometimes seemed to dominate the roads.

One day in Devizes I saw a huge flight of Horsa gliders, almost filling the sky. A single aircraft pulled three gliders, which were made of wood and fabric, and piloted by Army personnel. They were later used disastrously at Arnhem, when we invaded Holland. The Americans would never pass you by. I remember once a huge articulated transport vehicle stopped for me. The cab was full, "where do I get on?" I asked, "Hang on behind the cab" and I went to Avebury clinging on, keeping my feet away from the fifth wheel, where the trailer was connected on to the front end.

My parents sent on my bicycle, which I collected at Calne railway station. This made me more mobile for visiting pubs and cafés. I got friendly with a WAAF called Dora from a nearby camp at Wootton Basset, but unfortunately she got posted. One night a civilian policeman stopped me on the way back to camp for having no lights but 36-hour passes became available and a few of us soon realised that Bath was within the permitted travel radius, and that the Toc H took in servicemen. I got to like this and whenever possible I would cycle to Calne, catch a train to Bath (I always remember the porter shouting "train to Box, Corsham, Bath"), book in at Toc H have a meal, wander around then come back for the Saturday night dance. When the dance finished we cleared away any chairs and got out beds, blankets etc. and had a good nights kip. Sundays were often spent with the girls you'd met at the dance on the previous night. I made three particular friends, Hazel a WAAF from Coventry, Grace a WAAF from Chippenham and Iris Holtham a civilian who lived in Bath. Iris would come to the station with me on Sunday night for catching the last train back to Calne. She wrote to me for a long time after leaving Yatesbury and sent me magazines and papers when I was in India.

Routine life at the camp went on. Each morning the Orderly Corporal would come into the doorway of the hut and shout "any sick?" meaning who is going on sick parade to see the MO. The reply was always the same, "yes, I've got a bucket-full here". A gorilla of a man called Munn, whose grip really was vice-like, overstepped the mark one day, and was posted; I was pleased since I was in a bed near him, I think he was a psychiatric case.

After one week-end pass Ken Kidd got stranded in Swindon and walked all the way back to camp. It was early hours in the morning when he arrived and was charged with being AWOL. Next day, our F/Sgt, an old Chiefy whose name I forget, gave him a good talking to and let him off with the words "and don't you come 'ere absent no more". One day in Swindon, who should I bump into but my old friend Adrian (Taffy) Williams. We were delighted to see each other and met in Swindon quite a few times after that.

Organised games took place once or twice a week, usually football, which pleased a lot of the bods, but I skived off when it was foggy or frosty. One day the instructor said "anybody here play hockey?" Nobody did, but that didn't stop him; "right, here's 20 or more sticks, divide into two sides, and off you go." A dangerous hour and a half then passed, everybody swinging their sticks wildly, shins were bruised, but no first aid was needed. There was some drill, kit inspections, church parades and so on, only to be expected on a camp of this size. On the 14th October Queen Mary visited the camp. As the course was drawing to an end, we concentrated more on swatting, there being no text books of course; you had to rely on your own notes and no talking was allowed during these periods in the radar school. Written, practical and viva exams took place and I think most bods passed. We had been aware for some time that we were destined for Burma, or some region in South East Asia. This was confirmed when we were given medicals and inoculations for overseas postings. But we had 7-day passes and left Yatesbury on 20th December 1944 for Christmas at home.

CHRISTMAS 1944

This was a happy Christmas, with the family around me, I saw my old Lichfield Road pals, Alwyn Partridge, Jervis Littler, and Freddie Scott. The latter worked in a Bank and was not called up; Alwyn joined the Coldstream Guards and became a Sergeant drill instructor at Sandhurst Military College and Jervis an aircrew Sergeant wireless operator. I met up again with a girl named Betty Jones, who I had known since schooldays; she was a now a friend of my sister's, working together in the food office in Walsall Town Hall.

I also met Fred Hill for a drink or two, and he came over to Bloxwich for tea one afternoon. I delayed telling my mother that I was going overseas until Christmas was over, she was a bit worried when she found out.

OVERSEAS POSTING

4th January 1945. RAF Blackpool

Everyone knew that going to Blackpool meant kitting out with tropical gear. The uniforms and kit were stocked in the premises of Montague Burton of tailoring fame - hence the saying "going for a Burton" meant you were destined for an overseas posting. We were housed in billets with landladies still in occupation. Blackpool in wartime and midwinter was not an inviting place to be, but we were not there for long; instead of being kitted out I was posted, in transit, to Sutton Coldfield, a place I knew well, and near to Walsall.

6th January 1945.   RAF Sutton Coldfield, No. 216 MU

This was a big camp, just outside Birmingham. Quite a few old pals turned up, including Fred Hill. Duties were merely to accompany the driver of a stores lorry, which went every day round Erdington, Birmingham, Perry Bar and Sutton. Fred sometimes came as well, for the ride. I made quite a few visits home on a Walsall Corporation bus, a route I'd taken many times before to Sutton Park when still at school. There was a good NAAFI, and I soon made friends with several WAAFs who all happened to be in the WAAF band. Before I left Sutton Coldfield I'd had a date with every member of the band. But good times do not last, and I was posted again - back to Blackpool!

14th January 1945.   RAF Blackpool

I found myself in the same billet that I occupied before. There were some parades and lectures; one was on security, there was a National slogan at the time "Careless talk costs lives". But we were not kitted out and I was posted again.

16th January 1945.   RAF Morecambe

I arrived in Morecambe at 5.30 in the evening and was billeted, together with a Scots bod, in the house of a family called Fogg. There was mother (Alice) and a little girl and grandmother, the father away in the services. They treated us like sons. Alice even did some washing for me. I really was very touched by their kindness; there was no need to go out in the evenings. In any case, it was snowing and warmer inside. I wrote to the Foggs several times and I asked my mother send a gift, if she could find anything suitable, to the little girl. Alice wrote back to me, and to my mother, thanking us.

We were kitted out next day with tropical clothing, a second kit-bag, pith helmet and Sten gun. Every single item had to be marked with name and number using indelible ink; it took two or three evenings to do it all. Nevertheless, I still fitted in a visit or two to the cinema, and a few fish and chips suppers.

RAF SUTTON COLDFIELD

WAAF Band at Sutton Coldfield

TROOP SHIP

Troop ship 'Capetown Castle'

OUR DESTINATION

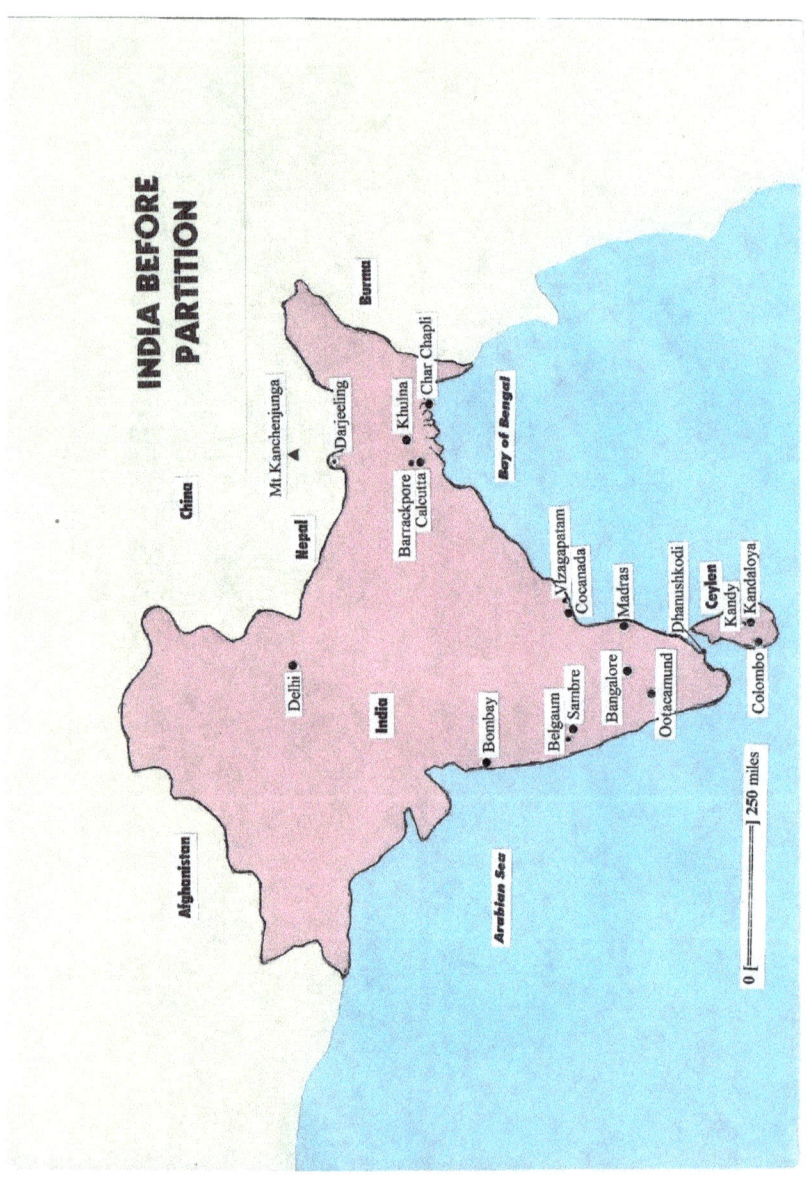

India before Partition

TO INDIA

22nd January 1945.   Troop ship "Capetown Castle"

The train took us to Bootle and after marching round the docks, I saw a huge ship looming up, blocking out the sky, as high as a block of flats. This was the "Capetown Castle", a cruise ship of the Union Castle line, now converted into a troop carrier. The gang plank only reached a level in the bowels of the ship, but we were herded into compartments which seemed to be about the size of a large living room. About 50 bods were crammed into each, but we had been relieved of our kit bags, which travelled separately. We were given hammocks. When slung, the hammocks were touching each other and the only way to cross the room was to bend double and stagger along underneath them. We were not allowed to get undressed at night. You had to carry your life jacket with you wherever you went. Eating was done in an adjacent room of similar size. The bods in there did not have hammocks; they had to sleep on the tables and benches (in style similar to what we see nowadays in picnic areas).

All the bods in our two rooms ate together so tightly packed on the benches that you couldn't use your arms; you sat with shoulders sideways, using wrist and head ducking movements for each 'mouthful (the situation improved somewhat at sea when lots of bods were up on deck suffering from sea-sickness). One bod from each mess table had to go into the bowels of the ship and collect food from the galley in cans. I remember mostly the undercooked rashers of tinned bacon for breakfast with hard-tack ship's biscuits. Most bods refused to eat these hard biscuits, but I quite liked them when dipped in tea. Washing and hygiene were a bit restricted and very communal, the "heads" (toilets) having no doors on them. The days were spent lounging around, eating chocolate and smoking cigarettes, which were cheap and in ample supply, and drinking tea. We lived like this for six days, moored to the quayside.

Eventually we cast off and a tug pulled us out to sea. A few civilians waved and we waved back. I remember we passed a moored-up RN destroyer with huge figures 723 painted on her side. I wondered if it was a good luck sign; I suppose it was, since I returned home unscathed. We were now free to roam the ship, although obviously a lot was out of bounds, such as galleys, officers 1st class, crew's quarters engine rooms, the bridge and many more. But roaming around meant you could meet up with old pals and it was gradually apparent that most of the radar bods from no.7 entry at the Northern Poly were on the ship, together with most of the bods from Yatesbury.

A lot of people were given jobs of some sort, and I was put in the baggage party. At first this meant going below decks when an officer requested his wanted-on-voyage trunk or case. The holds were very hot, and looking for the named-trunk was awkward in the dark with a little flash-lamp. One Czech officer, F/Lt. Hrbacek gave me a half crown when I took his case to his cabin I was quite taken aback when he insisted I take it. I got a glimpse of life on the 1st class decks; there were not only officers, but WAAFs and WRNS's of all ranks. It was said that most of those girls never saw much of India, since they were soon returned to the UK! Ship's crew I never saw - they must have been there somewhere.

As to our destination, when at sea we turned north instead of south; there were plenty of rumours of course but nobody really knew. We went round the north of Ireland and well into the Atlantic, as if going to America; it couldn't be there though, we'd got tropical kit in our no. 2 kit bags. In mid-Atlantic there were lots of other ships, mostly merchantmen, and we formed into a huge convoy with our ship and another troopship (the Orion) in the middle. We sailed towards Gibraltar with accompanying RN Destroyers zig-zagging around the convoy. Although at this time the war in Europe was going our way, the war was by no means won, and the German U-boats (sub-marines) were still active and dangerous. Now and then there would be a huge bang - in the hazy cold weather it was impossible to tell whether it was a depth charge or a gun, or whether in practice or in action. Eventually the convoy dispersed and we alone passed through the Straits of Gibraltar. We didn't see the Orion or any merchant ship again, but we saw many battleships of the Allied Navies moored in the beautiful Gibraltar harbour.

In the Mediterranean there was a more relaxed feeling, calmer sea, sea-sickness overcome except for George (Walky) Walkiden. He was sick all the way from Bootle to Bombay. I would sit beside him and when we saw flying fishes I said "cheer up Walky, what a sight, and all at HM Government's expense". He continued looking green. The weather was warmer and we were allowed to take our uniforms off at night and sleep in singlets and under-pants. Washing was not particularly refreshing; we were issued with sea-soap which was supposed to lather with sea water, which it didn't. At sea, taps, showers and toilets only ran sea water, and I always felt sticky after washing. Shaving soap didn't lather either. Four days after leaving Gibraltar we reached Port Said in rain, no sun and rather chilly. This continued as we sailed down the Suez Canal. We dropped anchor in the Gulf of Suez and were told that anybody who wanted could go for a route march in Port Tewfik.

Steel barges with steel covers containing fresh water came alongside and after discharging, we clambered on top, from rickety steps affair on the side of the ship. The barges were intended for carrying drinking water, not people, and there was nothing to hold on to. We jumped off at a derelict jetty and formed raggedy ranks, then shambled off along a kind of track in sand, rock and scrub. It suddenly became hot, and being unused to the heat being reflected off the ground, everyone soon started gasping, but we had to carry on. At last, in the middle of no-where, we came to a halt. In the distance I could see what appeared to be ship's decks and funnels gliding across the sand; of course, they were ships passing through the canal, their lower decks obscured by the sand banks. One ship was a troopship with Army bods going home - "Get yer knees brown" they shouted to us.

The reverse march and journey back to the ship was done in silence, everyone hot, sweaty, footsore, thirsty and dusty. One incident gave me the fright of my life before leaving Port Tewfik. I was lounging about on top of a pile of life rafts, stacked up as high as a house, when suddenly behind me there was a "whoosh, whoosh, whoosh", it was the most terrible noise I had ever heard, and was totally unexpected. It turned out that there was a rocket projectile launcher hidden behind the rafts, which no-one knew about. This was a practice or test firing, completely without warning.

Uneventfully, we sailed on down the Red sea, the Gulf of Aden and called in at the Port of Aden where a few bods disembarked. It was now getting really hot and we were told to change into tropical kit; it was two years before I saw my blue uniform again. We entered the Arabian Sea and engaged in some gunnery practice. This was with conventional guns, the target being a raft towed along by a RN vessel called HMS Baltimore. Long before we sighted the coast of India we could smell it. With Bombay in sight we hung around waiting for tug boats. Fred Hill had been admitted to the ship's hospital in the Red Sea and after a final visit, I helped him find his things as we were gliding alongside a dock in Bombay. Darkness had fallen and by now, lights on the ship were permitted.

As a member of the baggage party, I was called for duty to supervise the opening of the baggage holds, watch the kit bags and things being carried off on the heads of the dockers (about 100 of them, no cranes!)

and stacked in RAF lorries (from henceforth to be called gharries). Not knowing a word of Hindi I let the dockers get on with it, unless they did something really daft, when a howl of rage and waving the arms seemed to help. Each baggage party bod went off with a gharrie before general disembarkation, to a big hutted camp at Worli, where we supervised the unloading of the gharries as dawn was breaking.

24th February 1945.   RAF Worli, Bombay

Essentially a transit camp, RAF Worli was in a northern suburb of Bombay, flanked on one side by the sea and a nice promenade. There was no sand or beach however, but rather ugly weed-blackened rocks. I found my kit and a hut with a few empty charpoys, I bagged bed for myself and saved two for Fred Hill and Bill Paling, who had not yet arrived. Worn out and sticky after working through the night, I flopped down and went to sleep. The charpoy was the standard bed that looked the same all over India and beyond, I guess. It had a fairly sturdy wooden frame and legs, with interwoven ropes strung across in diagonal pattern. The rope was always rough and prickly, so for sleeping and to spread the load, a kind of heavy cotton mat was universally used as a "mattress". After continued use, the ropes stretched and wore and lying in this condition was like lying in a hammock; after extreme sagging it was exceptionally uncomfortable, hence when you arrived in a hut you always grabbed a charpoy with the tightest ropes. If there were only sagging charpoys, then it was hard luck, and you had to be alert for a quick grab when somebody was posted. Overhead wires were always provided to take your mosquito net, which could be thrown up during the day but had to be down and tucked in around your bedding mat at sunset.

After some tidying up, we all wandered around the huts looking for friends and acquaintances. We strolled along the promenade, which stretched for miles, and were plagued by Indian youths wanting to give manicures at grossly inflated prices. The promenade was lit at night by very efficient orange sodium-vapour lights, unseen at the time in England where blue mercury-vapour lamps were in use before the blackout. During our time in India, these lights were referred to (especially by Mac Sadler and Bill Paling) as "down the front at Worli lights". I believe Worli today is a fashionable and desirable residential district of Bombay.

We received mail and had another set of inoculations, despite having had them all in Morecambe a few weeks before. This was essential when changing from one Command to another (we were now in South East Asia Command). We handed in the pith helmets and were issued with bush hats, bedding mats and nets, anti-mosquito cream, sun glasses with leather side shields, a pocket jack-knife, sten guns (we'd only just handed those in on arrival!) and were paid in rupees and annas. I had one or two trips into Bombay on the electric train. One day in Bombay there was a religious-day puja, when everyone squirted coloured water on everyone else. They seemed to wear white clothes, presumably to show they had been thoroughly squirted with different colours. I bought a pillow and a bedding roll wrap, a sort of canvas sheet which, when rolled up, had two leather straps and a carrying handle. This was considerably more convenient than making your bedding up into little parcel with a length of rope; it also kept your bedding clean. After a few shopping trips and visits to the YMCA in Bombay, we were confined to camp while a lot of postings were carried out. I was posted to Ceylon (now named Sri Lanka), together with Fred, Bill, Walky, Mac and other friends from Northern Poly and Yatesbury.

BOMBAY

The YMCA

Entrance to Churchgate Street railway

A typical Bombay street

The Waterfront at Worli

View down the road

TO CEYLON

1st March 1945.   Troop train to Colombo

Early morning, mobs of us climbed into RAF gharries, laden with two kitbags, full webbing, water bottles, gas capes, bedding rolls, sten guns and what not!   At the station we were loaded into a waiting troop train. The layout of each carriage was conventional - corridor down one side, compartments for six people, toilet at each end (i.e. a hole in the floor with footprints marked so that you could position yourself correctly). The seats were made of wooden slats, as were the seat backs and the luggage racks.   For sleeping the seats served as two beds, the seat backs lifted up to make 2 more beds and the luggage racks provided two more. With six bods and their gear per compartment, movement was rather restricted, to say the least.   Our carriage was full of familiar faces and there was a lot of fun and joking but it was hot and we soon had aching bodies by sitting and sleeping on wooden slats.

Food consisted of American K rations (these were to pop up frequently over the next two years!).   Each meal was packed in a little cardboard box, covered in waxed paper, and marked B, L or D, i.e. for breakfast, lunch and dinner.   In each B box was a little tin of spam or cheese, some cheese biscuits, a sachet of instant coffee, some toilet paper and 3 cigarettes (usually Raleigh or Chesterfield - Camels were rarer and highly prized by non-smokers who bartered with them).   In the L and D boxes the coffee might be replaced by a sachet of bouillon powder (soup).   What to do with the sachets was a puzzle at first, but whenever the train stopped (frequently), bods hurried down to the locomotive and got boiling hot water from a little valve somewhere on the side and made hot drinks.   Otherwise, it had to be from your water bottle, treated with purification tablets.   At the stops, locals appeared as if by magic, selling dangerous looking sweetmeats and coloured water but of course, nobody risked these. In stations the vendors sold hard-boiled eggs, tangerines and bananas, which were welcome supplements, and char from "official" vendors was safe to drink. Children begging at every stop were a bit of a nuisance; at first we gave them oddments from our K rations or a few annas, but that only resulted in a bigger and noisier crowd. Mosquitoes were also a nuisance; nets could not be hung in the train, and the repellent cream was like sticky yellow Vaseline and nobody used it.

After zigzagging across Southern India, seemingly from one branch line and siding to another, we left the train at a big station in the large town of Trichinopoly. After a day there, which included a very hot route march, we boarded a primitive narrow gauge train, which was lousy with fleas, cockroaches, and other undefinable insects. The only food was hard-tack biscuits. Sleep was not possible and in the middle of the night, in the middle of nowhere, we left the train, and hung about in little groups. I relieved myself in a corner against a rock, and got a big surprise when it got up and walked away; it was either a cow or a buffalo, it was too dark to tell which. Some bods found a pile of old leaves (or so they thought) and decided to have a bonfire. After daybreak an officer in a foul temper was shouting that somebody had burned a local farmer's stock of plaited palm leaves (used for building "bashas" or huts) and was demanding compensation. An NCO came round and collected 25 annas from everybody. In daylight we could now see that this was Dhanushkodi, the ferry port at the tip of a promontory. A journey of 1000 miles had taken five days. We boarded the ferry which took us to an equivalent site in Ceylon, which was also a rail terminal, and a fairly respectable train took us into Maradana station, Colombo, in time for an evening meal.

6th March 1945.   Echelon Barracks, Colombo

At the station, instead of the usual RAF gharries waiting for us were three 60ft long trailers, open without sides. We scrambled aboard and clung on to whatever we could; in no time at all, my bush hat blew off. I shouted but the driver, 60ft away and in a separate cab, didn't hear. So for the rest of my time in Ceylon and India I never had a bush hat (two years later, on the boat coming home, some-one gave me one - too late!).   That evening I had two showers and a welcome change of clothes, a good meal at the All Services Club, and a nice cool stroll along the sea front.   Next morning we were told that none of our postings had come through, but we had to move out of the Barracks, which were right in the centre of Colombo.   Most of us went in gharries to Ridgeway, several miles out of Colombo.

7th March 1945.   RAF Ridgeway, No. 183 Wing

Here we handed in Sten guns and ammunition pouches, and thankfully there was a camp NAAFI.   There I bumped into George Tickell, an old friend from Northern Poly; we decided to hitch a lift into Colombo and go to the cinema. We missed the transport back and had to take a taxi. Next day, the MO gave some talks and yet another set of vaccinations and inoculations (we were in a new Command, namely Ceylon Air Forces).   Walky got a posting to Batticaloa, Mac to Negombo, and Fred to Galle.   I killed time by hitching into Colombo for cinemas and visiting the SWOC Club for some slap-up meals. At last, my posting came through, to Kandaloya - with Bill Paling.

19th March 1945.   RAF Kandaloya, 552 AMES

Bill and I left Ridgeway about mid-day on the back of an open RAF gharrie. Kandaloya was a tea plantation, elevation about 4,000 ft.   The MT driver told us, when we got there, that the winding undulating journey usually made people sick; we weren't, although we were bounced around a bit. After a hot bath and reading an Agatha Christie novel for relaxation, I wondered around admiring the views. One could see Negombo, 40 odd miles away, where Mac Sadler was posted. Also, Adams Peak was near, the highest mountain (8,280 ft.) in Ceylon. The domestic site was on sloping ground one side of the tea plantation. On the other side of the site was an escarpment, a sheer drop of about 1,000 - 1,500 ft. The road up to the site passed through the plantation where every day there were women with baskets on their backs picking the leaves.

The village where they lived was out of sight although at night we could hear their repetitious drums and pipes. Near the domestic site was a rocky area where a mountain stream flowed into a little tarn or pool, which was just about big enough to swim in, although very few people did, as it was so icy cold. On the camp, fires heated water for hot baths. There were wooden huts for accommodating and feeding about 20 bods. The cook house and mess doubled as a NAAFI at night and, when available, one could buy bottled beer from Canada and Cadbury's milk chocolate from New Zealand. There was an open badminton court and one could take lovely walks in beautiful scenery - and, unfortunately, leeches.

Nearly everybody who went walking would come back with leeches on their legs or in their boots. The domestic dogs, which never missed a good walk, always picked some up. Consequently, there were always leeches on the floors, mainly dropping off the dogs when full of blood. People treading on these inadvertently meant bloody floors, which was off putting, especially in the mess room. Many a time I helped bods to de-leech their legs by holding the lighted end of a cigarette under the leech, which caused it to withdraw its mouth from the flesh. Otherwise, pulling off would leave the leech's jaws embedded, resulting in a septic wound. In the huts were harmless little geckos (lizards) that ate other creepy-crawlies. It was said that if you caught one by the tail, he would shed it and run off, but I was never quick enough to try this out.

Leisure time was mainly spent writing letters or reading. Before long I received a batch of eight letters and some Walsall Observers. Occasionally a jeep would travel round the radar camps and give a film show. Fortunately, we had a generator and electric lights. Some evenings there was housey housey; I used to play crib with Bill. One day I hitched a ride into Kandy, the home of "The Temple of the Tooth". The scenery was breathtaking, with terraced paddy fields on the lower slopes of the mountains. On this trip I saw several wild elephants. But my diary says "Kandy is a lousy place".

The technical site was about 2,000 ft. higher than the domestic site and the journey was done by jeep. It was a dangerous journey, partly along the edge of the escarpment, with sheer 1,000 - 1,500 ft. drops. Many bends could not be taken in one turn, even in a jeep, and there had to be some backing and manoeuvring. It was even more tricky for the 15 cwt. Bedford that had to go up with stores and diesel fuel oil. One MT driver was so traumatised by the overhanging precipices that he had a nervous breakdown and was posted back home. The technical equipment was standard COL with a rotating aerial array on a gantry. The latter was on the highest peak, and while the gantry was only 40 ft. high, it turned my stomach going up there. But it was necessary to top up the hypoid oil in the gearing mechanism, and was all part of the DRM (daily routine maintenance). The same was true for the Lister diesels, or even worse, because on each shift there had to be a changeover from one of the two diesels to the other. Starting was the problem; there was a great big starting handle to swing, at the same time knocking a lever with your elbow to push in the decompression valves. It was exhausting but very pleasing when you heard the chug chug chug increasing in speed as it settled down. There were also two transmitters that had to be changed over and DRM to be done on the one taken off.

Being so high up we attracted much rain and thunder. Lightning was a real hazard; there were conductors to earth actual strikes, and discharge tubes to protect against static build-up. Sometimes these tubes were flashing all through the night. There was a land line to connect with the filter room in Trincomalee and this was often hit somewhere along the line. Rain and lightning was also very off-putting when climbing the aerial gantry; this job was put off as long as possible. One could get soaking wet moving about on the domestic site as well. I remember one bod coming out of the mess had his plate blown out of his hand by lightning. Actually, I didn't see too much of Bill Paling, as we alternated mostly on watch duties; we would swap a few words about faults and problems at the technical site, and then back in the jeep with the radar operators.

Towards the end of March I started receiving, in dribs and drabs, cablegrams with birthday wishes. This quite impressed the orderly room bods, as this was something new to them. Altogether I got nine cablegrams, five or six air mail letters, nine ordinary letters and several birthday cards. April 3rd was my 21st birthday, an ordinary day which I celebrated with Doc and Bill in the evening with lemonade and chocolate in the mess room. We also got some bad news - the station was to cease to be operational and put on C & M (care and maintenance). Bill and I thought about Fred, Mac, Walky and so on at the other radar stations, were they also closing?

We continued to go on watch and were ordered to dismantle the aerial and gantry turning gear (a bit more final than C&M, it seemed!). On the 8th April, the order was received for radar personnel (operators and mechanics) to return to Colombo; we organised a farewell party and left Kandaloya in gharries the next day.

10th April 1945.   Echelon Barracks, Colombo

Somehow or other I got separated from Bill and the others, and the only charpoy I could find was on a balcony overhanging a busy street. I was in full view of pedestrians and traffic, which was not too bad at night, but rather embarrassing getting up and dressing in the morning. I also got wet when it rained, which was frequent now that the monsoon had started. Later, I wandered round to the SWOC club and was delighted to find Bill, Fred and Mac already there. It turned out that all the radar stations had been put on C&M, and that all the crowd who arrived in Colombo five weeks ago were back there again. There followed a few days of socialising, eating and cinemas, but this comfortable life did not last long and we were on the move again.

TELEGRAM

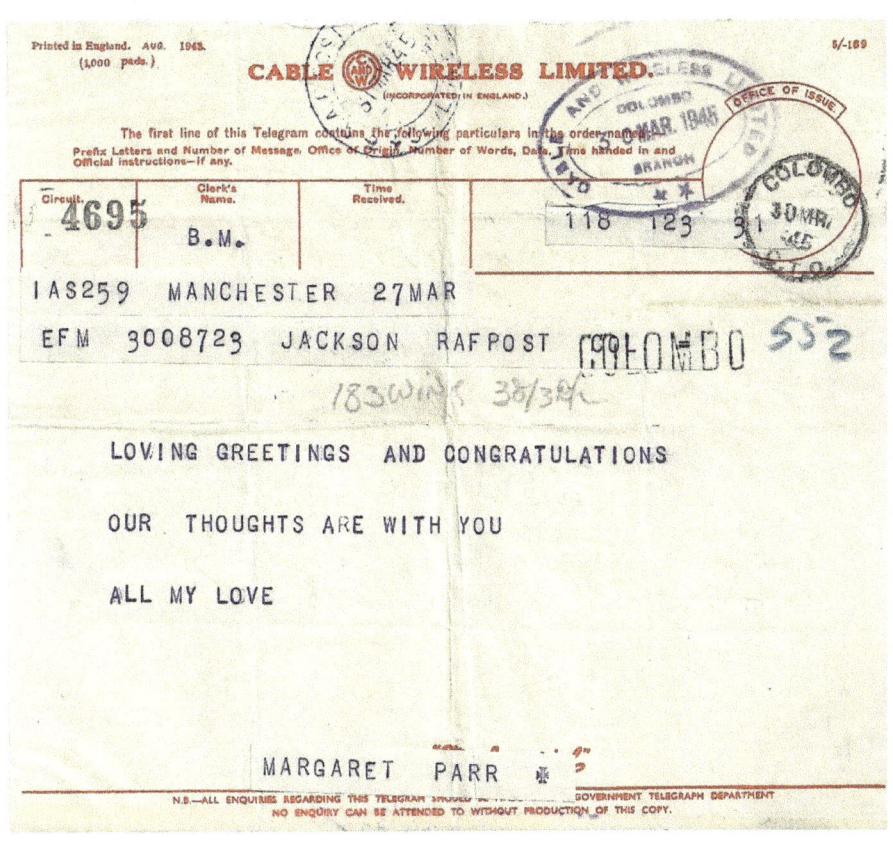

The cablegram received at RAF Kandaloya
for my 21st birthday, 3rd April 1945

TELEGRAM

Christmas telegram

13th April 1945.   Ratmalana No. 5 MRC

Several miles out of Colombo, this was a typical jungle Army camp, a Mixed Re-enforcement Company for British and Indian Army personnel. It was nearly empty, so RAF were in the majority. It consisted of bashas, huts made from interwoven palm leaves. The cookhouse was an open air affair and anything hot (or warm!) was heated on open wood fires, so char and food tasted strongly of wood smoke. Not that there was much food anyway. My appetite faded and the only thing I could stomach was wood-smoke flavoured runner beans out of a tin. It annoyed me one day when I was put on cookhouse fatigues for 24 hours, cleaning up and so on; I couldn't eat anything. I lounged about for a few days, writing letters and playing cards. Nearby there was a nice beach in a district called Mount Lavinia. I sometimes lay on the beach there, where you could get a dressed pineapple to eat, rather like eating corn-on-the-cob. It was very refreshing. Fred and I sometimes ate at the 'Hong Kong' restaurant there. The palm leaves bowed out towards the sea and nowadays, pictures of it appear in all the holiday brochures. Hotels have now sprung up there, with swimming pools and all mod cons.

We heard that, on the 26th April, Mussolini had been killed by Italian partisans and that his body had been publicly hung by its heels in a square in Milan. Three days later on the 29th April, Adolf Hitler and his mistress Eva Braun committed suicide by poisoning, whilst taking refuge from Russian troops advancing on Berlin.

We got lifts into Colombo on RN gharries (the Navy called them liberty boats). The SWOC club and cinemas were the main objectives. The buses in Colombo didn't go out to Ratmalana. They amused me greatly, they were all old double deckers, mainly Manchester Corporation and London Transport, still in their original (now faded) colours and with original route indicator panels. I don't know how they kept going, probably never having been serviced since the day they left England.   The road out of Colombo to Ratmalana went past the civic refuse dump and every time I had to hold my breath, the smell was so appalling.   Next to the dump was the City Maternity Hospital; I don't know how they survived.

Life dragged on, interspersed with route marches, night guard duties and other fatigues in an attempt to keep us occupied. One bod had caught "sleeping sickness" from a bite of a tsetse fly. He made us promise to continue shouting and shaking him each morning, as he was scared if left alone he would never wake up. He was waiting for a posting home. There were some poisonous millipedes in the bashas, shiny black with a red stripe.   These were best avoided; the glow worms were harmless, but were ugly big beetles in daylight. Fireflies swarmed under the trees at night, but again were like big horse - flies when seen in daylight. At dusk there were also big lizards around, a sort of iguana perhaps, and these were best left alone. We were not sorry to move on when postings came through.

BACK TO INDIA

1st May 1945.   RAF Sambre, No. 7 BSU

I left Ratmalana at 5 a.m. in a gharrie to Maradana station and the train took me to the ferry point. I don't remember the circumstances, but I was separated from my pals again. It was dark on arrival and I slept on the beach. Up again at 5.0 a.m. and I boarded a very small ferry boat with a mob of sullen Japanese Prisoners of War. I arrived at Dhanushkodi about midday, had a dip in the sea and some lunch. Then I waited until 7.0 p.m. for the narrow gauge train to Trichinopoly. For every stage of a journey there is always more waiting than travelling. After a 24 hour wait in Trichinopoly I caught a train to Bangalore; a 27 hour wait there, then I caught a train at 1.00a.m. to Belgaum. This town was several miles inland from Goa, a Portuguese colony at the time and now a popular tourist resort. Belgaum was the nearest rail town to where I was going, a village called Sambre, where no.7 Base Signals Unit was stationed. The journey had taken just over five days.

Sambre itself was a primitive village, an unhygienic collection of tumble-down bashas, outside wood fires and no amenities. It was located directly adjacent to the Western Guardroom of the main camp, where there were some large trees housing up to 100 flying foxes. These were large fruit eating animals that hung upside down all day, their droppings being quite unpleasant. They swarmed out of the trees with loud squeaking noises each evening looking for food. Sometimes families of large baboons would come sweeping down from the trees as raiding parties, looking for tit-bits.

No.7 BSU was a large camp divided into three sites. 'A' site was really a camp in itself, with brick billets, full messing facilities, sterilised drinking water tanks, administration block, a flagpole, library, cinema, dhobi -

and a tented site where new arrivals, including me, were accommodated. 'B' site was an airfield several miles away, with a squadron of fighter planes. 'C' site was a relatively short walk away from 'A' site, a GCI radar station, No.863 A.M.E.S., with tented accommodation. A.M.E.S. was the abbreviation for Air Ministry Experimental Station, the word Radar never being used.

The 'A' site tents, several hundred of them, had concrete floors with four charpoys squeezed into each tent. With four people inside with kit bags etc., and not enough height to stand upright, it was a cramped existence. Somehow or other I met up again with Bill Paling and we were put into a tent with two other bods (strangers).

The mess rooms and toilet blocks were divided into groups, one group for BORs (British Other Ranks) and IORs (Indian Other Ranks), but showers and other amenities were communal. At first, the daily routine was a roll call parade, a route march every now and then and lounging about on one's charpoy. The mess rooms were converted into recreation rooms after the last meal of the day, where you could sit and write letters; I kept some blotting paper for this purpose, to avoid wetting the writing paper with sweat from my wrists. There were no Biro's or ball-pens then, it was ink and fountain pen. A cherished possession was a Parker 51; you could put your name down for one, but I was never lucky in a draw.

On the 8th May after a route march we were told of victory in Europe and given the rest of the day off. Next day there was a big Church Parade, after that nothing happened, so we continued lounging until an NCO came round and collared a few of us for a night guard duty. I thought we'd escaped more jabs, but no, we were in a new Command, namely South East Asia Air Forces, changed to India Command later in the year. We also had medicals, and I was passed fit for mobile and assault. We knew what was in the wind as we now had some concentrated weapon training, firing rifles, stens and Browning machine guns, throwing grenades, going through gas with masks and protective clothing on, and bayonet practice.

One day, the weapons instructor didn't turn up; a few of us got fed up after an hour of hanging about and went for an early lunch. After we had gone he came and had a roll call; we were arrested and charged, I don't remember what with, and marched one at a time under escort to be sentenced by the Adjutant. I got three days jankers that meant confined to camp, parading at set hours at the guardroom and doing marching or odd jobs in the cookhouse or anywhere else where a few dirty jobs were waiting to be done. Normal weapons training and assault courses continued, including "jungle penetration". For this we were taken out at sunrise in gharries to a hilly region 14 miles on the other side of Belgaum; it was covered in trees, scrub and gorse and we played follow my leader. Alas, not so easy as it sounds. We were given blank ammunition to fire if we got lost. We were taught about survival, and how to cool off in a brook or mountain stream, i.e. roll up your sleeves and only immerse your wrists in the water. It really does work. By sunset we were shattered and could only lie on our charpoys when we got back to camp. But we later heard that the Army landed unopposed in Burma and the accent on weapon training slowly faded. One day there was a big parade of all the bods from 'A', 'B' and 'C' sites and I found myself marching in a group of bods that I'd never seen before. We halted, did a right turn and who was beside me but a man from Bloxwich, not far from where I lived, and knew well. His name was Arthur Rodgers. He was as surprised to see me as I was to see him. We couldn't speak, the parade went on, was dismissed and I never saw him again.

At the end of May, Bill Paling had to go into a Military Hospital near Belgaum. Returning to the tent I was surprised to find an IOR in his charpoy. But he was a nice chap and we got on very well. He was a

Sikh and I was intrigued when he unwrapped his RAF blue turban at night. His wispy long hair was in a bun, over which he put a sort of hair net, and then a kind of bag round his jaw to hold his beard. I marvelled at the way he so accurately wound his turban back on in the mornings. His mother used to send him food parcels in little basins; he always gave me some and it was quite nice. I visited Bill in hospital several times, but he didn't come back to Sambre, instead he was posted to Worli. I thought this meant repatriation and that I wouldn't see him again, but he remained in India and I did see him again!

Towards the end of June the monsoon started in our region, and we were issued with monsoon capes. They were very acceptable as it was very wet walking to and from 'C' site. We were now spending nearly all our time up there and when some of the lads were offered tents to live there they accepted with alacrity. But I'd had enough of tents and those at 'C' site only had dirt (mud!) floors. The cookhouse was more like a field kitchen and I'd had a bellyfull of that at Ratmalana. Some NCO's lived there too, (best avoided) and with the monsoon just breaking I took the opportunity to move into a good brick billet on 'A' site. I was up at 'C' site every working day anyway, and could still play monopoly, Kan-u-go and battleships and cruisers with my pals.

The radar work at 'C' site was humdrum. The kites from 'B' site never flew, so there was nothing to track. Bods were even volunteering for work to break the monotony; Fred went to Secunderabad on a waterproofing course (i.e. waterproofing of radar vehicles for landing by sea); Mac and Taffy Payne went to Bangalore; Les Price went somewhere for radar-carrying landing craft familiarisation; I saw the Education Officer about going on an EVT instructors course and filled in application forms (EVT stands for Education and Vocational Training, a new branch apparently set up after the cease-fire in Europe).

By the beginning of August all the bods who went on courses were coming back and Bill Paling, Walky, Hassy and Middlemass turned up. Most of them went to 'C' site, but I remained at 'A' site; I had a bearer who did all my odd jobs, mainly fetching and carrying char or my dhobi, making beds and polishing shoes. He was a Christian and would eat and smoke any given quantity, but a trustworthy old boy.

SAMBRE "A" SITE

Flagpole at Station HQ

Dhobi gat (wash house) in the north sector.
Brick admin buildings in background

Herd of goats outside "A" site.
Guardroom on the right

Camp Chapel
Formerly a
parachute store

Camp Cinema on right

Surplus charpoys in Barracks Store as
RAF Sambre begins to close

SAMBRE "C" SITE

Les Price and his radar goose
("The Good Ship Venus")

The Lister diesel generator for 863 AMES at "C" site

Christmas at "C" site. Mac Sadler, George Johnstone, Taffy Payne, Trevor Dunne and ?

723 Jackson by gharrie - 723

About this time, Belgaum town that had been out of bounds to BOR's and IOR's, became unrestricted. So we frequently caught the bus for jaunts to the Globe cinema and the Meade Club. Belgaum itself was a dump with a dirt main road, open gutters and drains, and shops more like market stalls selling nothing you wanted to buy. One shop actually had a glass front window, a sort of House of Fraser in miniature. It sold fancy goods, wines and spirits but only sergeants and officers were allowed to go in, so for us it was tea and cakes and ping pong at the Meade Club.

The buses were really quaint; they had Indian built bodies on American Chevrolet or Diamond 'T' chassis and were fuelled by gas from a charcoal burner hanging at the back. I never fathomed how this worked, but before setting off the driver would fan the fire, pipes and tubes got hot and then the bus moved off and gathered speed, without being set alight. It was always overcrowded of course; I always seemed to end up sitting between two big fat Indians, preparing from a banana leaf some betel nut and lime (calcium oxide, not the fruit) for chewing on the journey. This stained their teeth red and when they spat out the debris on the floor, it made a gory-looking mess. What with the Globe cinema and the camp cinema, it seemed that I went to the pictures nearly every day. Bill, Fred and I had our photographs taken one day at a good Indian photographic studio in Belgaum.

During July, we heard that Russia had declared war on Japan; and on 7th August the Americans dropped the first atom bomb on Hiroshima. On the 15th August, Emperor Hirohito persuaded the Japanese Government to surrender; and on the 2nd September, General MacArthur formally received the Japanese capitulation on board the American war-ship USS Missouri. Earl Mountbatten, who was chief of operations in Burma, on the 2nd September accepted the surrender of 750,000 Japanese troops in his area of command at a formal parade in Singapore. All this news, which came to us belatedly in dribs and drabs, cheered us up no end, because the end of the war in Europe meant little to us.

In an RAF magazine called 'Airflow', modelled around Lilliput, a very popular pocket magazine of the time, I came across an amusing little ditty:-

> *Brain dumb,*
> *Inspiration won't come,*
> *Can't write, bad pen,*
> *Best wishes, Amen.*

Fortunately, whenever I settled down to write letters I could find plenty to say and to thank the people who had written to me. I was lucky to get a lot of mail, from UK and internal, I even got one from Hank Hemming from Skegness days. We could by now write "uncensored" letters using Green Envelopes or Blue Triangle Air Letters. These of course, were rationed. They could also be used internally as for example, when Bill Paling wrote to me at RAF Sambre from RAF Karachi.

We were getting more and more odd jobs at 'C' site. The chief offender was a corporal Farley, a Geordie whose accent grated on me. (But I must say that many years later, when visiting foundries in the North East, I met dozens of Geordies who were grand blokes and I quite enjoyed their accents). The GCI station, 863AMES, had its components mounted in separate gharries; we found that when the diesel was running, switching the transmitter on caused a sudden load on the diesel, whereupon a cloud of black smoke was emitted from the exhaust. This was used as a signal to those lolling around that Cpl. Farley was on the prowl.

Chaddy by this time had tired of the xylophone he started to make on the Capetown Castle and was now constructing a one-string violin. But some of us had to put up poles for a telephone line between 'C' and 'A' sites and I had to put up electric lights in the field kitchen when a surplus petrol electric generator (Peggy) became available. We painted the aerial arrays, erected platforms between the gharries, and I tried exterminating ants with fuel oil. (In India, perishable food was always kept in "meat safes" with their legs standing in tins of oil, which prevented ants from climbing up). It suddenly dawned on us that as AC.2's of long standing, the lowest rank with lowest pay, we ought to seek betterment. So we asked Cpl. Farley if he would organise a Trade Test Board, with a view to being upgraded to AC.1's. He hummed and hawed because, I think, he was wary of being appointed the examiner. We had no notes or text books, so we refreshed our memories by questioning each other and instead of playing hangman or battleships and cruisers, we busied ourselves with drawing circuit diagrams and writing notes on di-poles, selsyns, maintenance and so on.

Eventually, we got the written exams and vivas over (an officer supervised the Board, with a sergeant) and on 21st September Fred, Mac and I became AC.1's with a small increase in pay (there were others too, but I didn't record their names in my diary).

Bubonic plague broke out in the district and Belgaum was put out of bounds again. We all had inoculations against bubonic and yellow fever. My bearer was dismissed, as he had contracted sceptic scabies. We had some instruction on a T63 Early Warning Unit but there was no spark (!) of interest. Mac and I applied for leave in the Nilgiri Hills and our application was successful.

BELGAUM

723 Jackson taken in a Belgaum studio

Rex Cinema

Meade Club

Hotel Green, for Officers only

Belgaum Church

KEEPING IN TOUCH

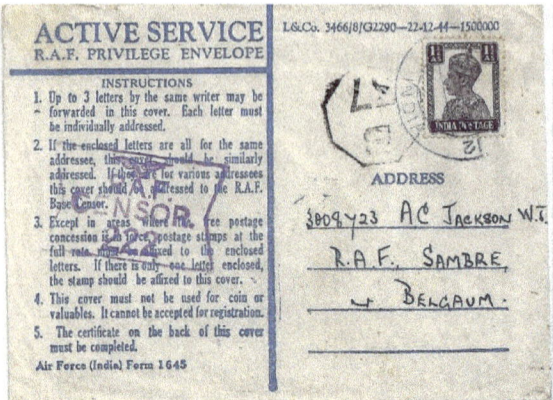

Typical covers for un-censored letters

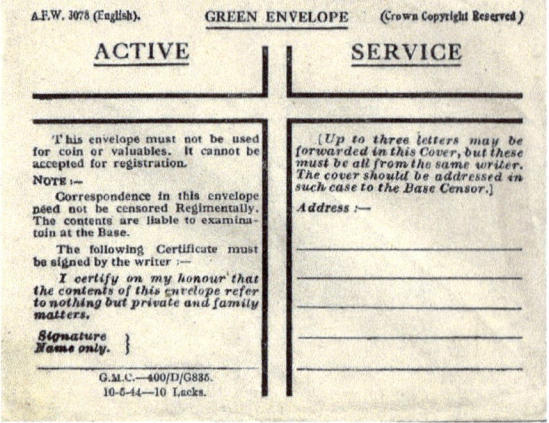

A stamp was required for internal mail

TRAVELS IN INDIA

31st October, 1945. Wellington Barracks, Ootacamund

We left Belgaum station at midnight and arrived in Bangalore 24 hours later. Why do all these journeys take place at midnight or the early hours? We had to cross Bangalore for the journey to Jalarpet and had to sleep there and wait until afternoon for a train to Coimbatore. We arrived there at 1.0 o'clock in the morning and had to wait there all day for a train to Mettupailyam. There we had to change for the mountain railway, which was rack and pinion on the steeper parts through Coonoor and up 2650 feet to Ootacamund. We finally got to the camp at Wellington at 11.0 o'clock at night, thoroughly worn out, a three-day journey of only 200 miles, bitten by bugs and having eaten only K rations. We drew blankets from the stores and flopped down.

There wasn't really much to do on the camp or in the towns of Ootacamund and Coonoor. Ooty had been the fashionable place to go for the old burra sahibs and the old club house there was more of a museum. We hired bikes to get around, but hill cycling was very tiring. The most common diversion was the cinemas - the Vincent Talkies, the Bedford Talkies and camp cinema. The films, here and everywhere else, were mostly American trash.

The trouble with Hill Stations is that they attract rain and many days it just poured down non-stop all day. I suppose that is why tea plantations thrive in hilly regions. Two visits were very good however, one to a silk-worm farm and the other to a tea processing and packing station in a big tea plantation. The tea was grown for home consumption and not sold outside India. However, they were willing to send personal packages to the UK and my mother and family said it was the nicest tea they had ever tasted. From Ooty I also sent back home some food parcels and some towels, linen and shirt material, all on ration in England. I caught a cold, the first in India, and was happy to be returning to Sambre; again it was a bug and flea ridden journey of 3½ days.

20th November 1945. RAF Sambre, No.7 BSU

We got back to Sambre and resumed the usual routine and odd jobs at 'C' site, including bomb dump guard and cookhouse duties. I also sent some more parcels home, mainly shoes. By drawing the outline of a foot and sending a picture of a style from a magazine, the shoe wallah made very good shoes which were much appreciated at home in times of shortage. I also had some shoes and chaplis (sandals) made for myself. Relief from Cpl. Farley's little jobs came when I was sent on detachment to Bangalore for EVT instructor assessment.

OOTY HOLIDAY

Lower Coonor, the Indian half of the town

Mountain railway, almost at Coonor

Mountain railway up to Ootacamund

15th December 1945.   RAF Adgodi, No.3 EVT School (No.51 RS)

RAF Adgodi, just outside Bangalore, was essentially a Radio School but part of it had been turned into an EVT training school. I was pleased to find there Ron Middlemass an old mate from the Northern Poly, and two bods who were in my class at Yatesbury (rather odd types). I quickly found the camp cinema and took Middlemass to the Imperial cinema and Chinese Victory café in Bangalore, which I already knew. The course was relaxing, an easy-going officer in charge. We received lectures on teaching, taking part in discussion groups and giving lectures. A fair amount of time was spent preparing for the latter. I gave a talk on "The action of water on metals" but I haven't the faintest recollection what I said, or what my other lectures were about.

Christmas day came, and in the morning I went on my own into Bangalore to the Methodist Church there, a fine big airy building with wicker chairs all spotlessly clean. Back at camp we had a good Christmas lunch, the BOR's being served by the Sergeants (an RAF tradition). I hitched a ride on an army gharrie afterwards and went to the open air roller skating rink. It was strangely very quiet in Bangalore.

One day strolling around and wearing my new 'snogging' suit (a military style tailored suit in good quality khaki drill), who should I bump into but my old pal Adrian (Taffy) Williams of Northern Poly days. We spent quite a lot of time together, walking in the parks, going to cinemas and restaurants. I recollect seeing, somewhat grudgingly I must confess, Italian ex-prisoners of war strolling around in smart 'snogging' suits with plenty of money in their pockets.

Before leaving Adgodi, my bearer stole all my money from under my pillow whilst I was taking a shower. It was quite a large sum (about Rs 70 I think) so I went straight to the guardroom and reported my loss.

The SP's instantly dismissed him, but the money was never recovered. After an end-of-course party, we said goodbye to each other and got movement orders for return to unit, not knowing if we'd passed or failed.

12th January 1946.   RAF Sambre, No.7 BSU

Waiting for me back at Sambre there were 14 letters, six bundles of magazines and 30 copies of the Daily Mail. I went up to 'C' site for social visiting; Mac and Les Price had now "got" a gharrie and they ran me back to 'A' site at night. I mostly mooched about, playing badminton, and I asked the EVT officer if he knew of the results of the Adgodi course. He didn't, but he gave me a job in the library to help pass the time. There were no parades, so social visits to 'C' site and Belgaum were the order of the day. We got wind of a possible Trade Test and started again some mutual swotting. The test was very low key when it came; an officer called F/O Binge (what a name!) asked me to draw a block-diagram (not even a circuit diagram) of a superheterodyne receiver, checked it over and told me that I'd passed. So I was now an LAC (Leading Aircraftsman) which didn't mean much, but I got a small increase in pay, how much I don't recall. Lots of bods were leaving Sambre and I was signing their clearance chits on behalf of the library. One I signed for was Sgt. Freddie Mills, a PT Instructor in the RAF and professional boxer in civilian life. We had watched him give several demonstration bouts inside the camp cinema. He died under mysterious circumstances in the late 1940's.

We got a visit from General Auchinlek, but there was no 'bull' or parade. 'C' site closed and all who lived there moved to the billets in 'A' site. Then we heard that No.7 BSU had been disbanded (anything to do with the General's visit?) and would now be addressed as No.7 BSU Detachment. Even more bods were leaving Sambre and surplus charpoys were piling up. All the library books that I had classified and crated were sent away (to where, I don't remember). All the radar mechanics were posted to units in Calcutta, Kuala Lumpur, Vizagapatam, Bangkok, and one to Hanoi in Indo-China (now Vietnam), leaving behind Johnny Johnstone, Mac Sadler, Les Price, Archie Young and me.

They closed Billet 13 and I had to move to Billet 32 - what an upheaval! Then Archie and I were posted to RAF Cocananda, 23012 A.M.E.S. It so happened that Mac and Les had volunteered to be drivers in a convoy of vehicles going to Madras, so Archie and I volunteered to go with them as co-drivers, even though Madras was in the opposite direction to Cocanada. We got cleared, then our movement orders and travel warrants, and nobody seemed to mind.

BANGALORE

Showing off my new "snogging suit" in
Cubbon Park, Bangalore

Commercial Street, the main shopping street

A road off Commercial Street

Russell Market, Bangalore

Myself, Middlemass and ? outside
our billet at Adgodi, Bangalore

Modern architecture, St Joseph's College

Part of the Mysore Government Secretariat, Bangalore

Old architecture, a Hindu Temple

23rd February 1946. RAF Madras

We left Sambre at 10.30am. Les Price, who always had an eye for a good vehicle, bagged a Ford V8 Light Warning vehicle (no.7 in the convoy) and I travelled with him. Mac Sadler got a big Crossley Transmitter vehicle (no.5, labelled Mac's Crate) and Archie Young went with him. Eight of the vehicles soon broke down and by 9.30pm we had only reached a Staging Post at Harihar. We washed off the dust and sweat, pitched our tents, and it was after midnight when I got to bed. Next day, we towed the broken-down gharries into an Indian Army I.E.M.E. station for repair and spent the rest of that day just hanging around. The following morning we left Harihar and travelled the 180 miles to Bangalore. Les let me do some driving and kept a very close eye on me.

One vehicle got involved in a crash, but we arrived safely about 5.30pm (villagers threw stones at RAF and Army gharries). We parked at No.225 Group Transit Camp on the outskirts of Bangalore. Mac, Archie, Les and I went in our V8 to Bangalore for some Chinese food, and then to the New Opera cinema. The next four days were spent in and out of Bangalore, eating mainly at the Chinese Victory Café, I took my wrist-watch in for repair and we collected 300 gallons of petrol. On 2nd March the convoy left Bangalore under a Military Police escort (I don't remember why). Before leaving we went into a WVS canteen for Ovaltine, cream horns and chocolate cakes, knowing that we would be eating K rations for the rest of the day. At Ranipet the Staging Post was closed, but the WVS let us sleep on tables and chairs in the canteen and they kindly provided us with breakfast in the morning.

Another day of travelling in the V8, and the convoy arrived at Madambakkam, where Les and Mac had to leave all the vehicles. We had travelled 400 miles. I went into Madras, ate at the YMCA and then went to a cinema. I bumped into two radar mechanics I knew at Sambre (Eddie Cloke and Ivor Tutt). They had been posted to Malaya, but on the journey their posting was cancelled and they had ended up in Madras. I had been staying in a Transit camp at Tambaram but I got on an RAF gharrie to Madras Central Station, met up with Archie Young, and Mac and Les, who came down from Madambakkam on the suburban electric train. We got an evening mainline express train, destination Calcutta, which Archie and I left at Cocanada Port. We bid Mac and Les fond farewells.

SAMBRE-MADRAS CONVOY

Convoy stops for dinner. Our gharrie has number 7 on the back

Archie Young and Les Price by "Mac's Crate" at Harihar

Les Price, Mac Sadler and ?
cooling off at the roadside

Les Price and I by the V8 that we took to Madras

Myself, Les Price and Mac Sadler by "Mac's Crate", starting off from Sambre

MADRAS – CALCUTTA EXPRESS

Les Price and Mac Sadler leaning out of the window, waiting for the bearer to bring breakfast

Typical desolate countryside viewed from the
Madras-Calcutta train

A view from the Madras - Calcutta train near Bezwada

6th March 1946. RAF Cocanada, 20312 A.M.E.S

Cocanada is a coastal town and hence, very hot. Temperatures were 112° F (45°C) in the shade and 120°F (50°C) in the sun. Radio Madras said that Cocanada was the hottest place in Southern India. I think it was here that I started taking mepacrine, a yellow anti-malaria tablet that turned your skin yellow. It was not an option; once told to take them you had to continue, or else! The domestic site at Pagadelapetta was made up of bashas, about three miles out of Cocanada, the technical site being another one or two miles further on and next to the sea. The shore line was dirty and smelly and the locals harvested salt there, by building lagoons of sea water which evaporated in time, leaving a mixture of salt and sand (that was why the table salt in the mess was so gritty!) So nobody bothered with the sea and for swimming used the Forces Club open air pool, near to an Army Camp a few miles away. We drew our provisions from there; in India, the RAF had to buy from the RASC (Royal Army Service Corps.) and we often complained that we got second best. But it was handy, as the provisions gharrie could drop off any bods wanting a swim. The open air cinema was also at that camp, but at nights there was a special liberty run. One day the provisions gharrie driver came back looking a bit white; he had hit a monkey and was immediately surrounded by a mob calling for his blood. Monkeys (and all apes) have the right of way on the road, like the Brahmin cows, and there is a religious association to their well-being.

The radar station was one in the East India Loran chain, with sites in Madras, Cocanada, Vizagapatam, Char Chapli and Chungking (China). The chain was built by the Americans for flight navigation purposes. They had abandoned the one in Chungking because of the civil war in China. There, Mao Tse Tung and his Red communists were fighting the established Chinese government under Chang Kai Shek, and destroying anything to do with Western Civilisation. The Americans had withdrawn from the area and were concentrated on fighting in the

Pacific, and had handed over the remaining four Loran stations to the RAF. It was of course, all American equipment, about which I knew nothing. I had to learn pretty fast, so I made a few trips to the technical site to see how the other radar mechanics were handling it. Fortunately, one of these was Ron Johnson who I knew from Yatesbury days, and he was very helpful. The C.O. was a F/Lt. Bannerjee, an Anglo-Indian, who sat in his basha all day, never leaving the camp to my knowledge. He was despised by other Indians (all half-castes were) and was afraid to venture out.

The gear itself was relatively simple, there being no moving parts as in the case of COL and GCI. It was housed in Quonsett huts, the American equivalent of Nissens. Three things caused annoyance however. Firstly, there was no land-line link to Vizagapatam, the master station; there was radio contact, the transmitting aerial being of the Beveridge type, stretching like a very long washing line out of the perimeter fence on to the shore. This was a godsend to the locals, some lovely copper wire at head height, there for the taking! Secondly, the diesel generators. These were American and could not be started manually. Banks of nickel-iron batteries powered a starter motor, and if the engine failed to start the batteries soon went flat. Panic would then set in and connections changed over to the diesel already running in order to give the batteries a booster charge. Often half the watch was spent fiddling about in this manner. Furthermore, the governors were faulty and the engines raced which played havoc with the radar gear (fuses and valves), which had to be kept in sync with the other stations in the chain. We had a visit from Jock Howie who was now attached to the MRDU (Mobile Diesel Repair Unit) but all he could do was recommend replacing one or more of the three American diesels with British Listers - a good decision I thought.

Thirdly, at night we had dimmed lighting so as not to interfere with the operator's watching the screens. This seemed to be just the right level for attracting big green grasshoppers or crickets; they would swarm into the hut in hundreds. The receivers were in a cage of fine wire mesh for electrical screening and the night lights were inside the cages to allow the operators to see, make notes, etc. The outside of the cage would be absolutely covered with these large insects, clicking as they jumped about, getting on your clothing and everywhere. If everything was otherwise quiet, the mechanics would sit outside altogether. If there was only one operator, I would go inside the cage and help him.

At the domestic site there was another annoyance - water. The water bowser was a relatively small tank on two wheels. It soon became empty, and for some reason, there was nearly always a delay in taking it to be refilled. Being without water even for a whole day was worse than it sounds and in such high temperatures, prickly heat soon appeared if one could not wash. The single shower was beside the bowser; to get water up into an overhead bucket, there was a little reciprocating hand pump which had to be yanked to and fro for ages to get enough water up. There were howls and curses when the water dried up.

April 3rd came, another birthday. I was on watch in the morning and went downtown Concanada in the afternoon, but everything was closed as it was New Years' Day, according to one religious calendar. I was back on watch at 11.00pm so it was a very quiet birthday.

Four days later I was posted to AHQ (Air Headquarters) Secretariat Section, Delhi and collected my movement order and rail ticket warrant.

CONCANADA

Some of the bods from 23012 AMES by
the swimming pool at the forces club

My cat by my basha at the domestic site

Quonsett hut housing the radar gear at
the technical site

Ron Johnson cooling off at
Pagadelapetta

Technical Site at Pagadelapetta

Loran transmitting mast

Hindu shrine at Pagadelapetta

Hindu temple at Pagadelapetta

8th April 1946. RAF AHQ Delhi

I left Cocanada in the early hours of the morning on the 8th April and arrived in Delhi in the morning of the 12th April, a journey of about 800 miles. I had to go to RAF Vizagapatam first, for clearance and pay. I spent the night there (and went to the camp cinema of course). I changed trains again at Bezwada where I had to join a troop train. A typical evening meal was hard tack and bully beef (almost molten), for breakfast hard tack and one tangerine. We did get an ice allowance however, to cool our water bottles. We stopped at Nagpur and Bhopal where some of the Army bods left the train; it gave us a bit more space and the opportunity to buy char and more tangerines.

On arrival I reported to AHQ Secretariat Section which was a remarkably fine building put up by the British Raj in peace time. Nobody knew, or wanted to know, anything about me, but as I wandered from one office to another, who should I bump into but Fred Hill, so I gave up and went back with him to his billet. I dumped my kit and had a good shower after 4½ days in the heat. The billet was in an ex-American Army camp, and there were flushing toilets, the first and last I ever saw in India. In the evening, we went to a cinema!

Next day I found an EVT officer and reported to him. But he didn't show much interest, so I didn't bother with him again. I wandered around New Delhi on my own, admiring the magnificent buildings and the grand open spaces with grass and trees. I'm sure it would not have been like this if the British hadn't been there. Old Delhi was out of bounds, but that didn't bother me. I did some shopping, bought some ladies shoes for sending home, went to a cinema each evening and made a few new pals. It was very hot, I don't recall the temperatures, but there were posters in English advising Servicemen where to get free salt tablets, in order to avoid heat exhaustion. With that you can become a hospital case, as you can with sunstroke. Scrawled all over the downtown area were the words "Jai Hind", colloquially meaning "Quit India" and aimed of course, at the British.

At last I found an office which had my records, and the movement order was a mistake; so I had to return to Cocanada. I got the usual necessities, such as travel warrant, booked a gharrie to the station and said goodbye to Fred Hill. On Good Friday I left the camp at 7.00am and at Delhi Junction station was told the train left at 8.20pm, not 8.20am. I spent the day at the Wavell Canteen eating doughnuts, ice cream and drinking iced lime juice. The train proved to be a troop train from Lahore full of IOR's. It was another uncomfortable journey to Bezwada, sleeping up on the third tier, and noisy since some of the Indians had monkeys, drums and tom-toms. I eventually got to Cocanada Port, having been away for only 15 days, although it seemed much longer. At least, I had the opportunity of being a tourist in New Delhi!

DEHLI

One of the domes of the Secretariat building

Legislative Assembly

New Delhi railway station

Connaught Circus, the main shopping area
(one complete circle)

Temple in Old Delhi

RETURN TO CONCADA

Movement Order and Rail Warrant from AHQ
India. Delhi to Concanada Port

23rd April 1946.   RAF Cocanada, 20312 AMES

Looking around for some RAF transport, I could see none. A friendly civilian advised me to catch a rail car to Cocanada Town, which was nearer to the RAF camp. I waited on another platform with a mob of locals and eventually an ancient-looking diesel rail car rolled up. I was encumbered with all my kit and by the time I'd collected my thoughts and my kit, the rail car was filled and covered with the locals, on the roof and hanging on the sides. The driver, who sat in a tiny cab, said I could get in with him, so I squeezed myself and kit alongside him, and we creaked and clattered along the single track branch line. At Cocanada Town there was no RAF gharrie in sight, so I got a tonga to the camp.

Cocanada was just as hot as ever, even hotter it seemed, than Delhi. After getting adjusted, and back in my old basha, I was very pleased to receive a parcel from my sister Margaret with some table salt (a real luxury to have salt without sand), and some other items I had requested, including shampoo, buttons and darning wool. The Indian civilian cook was still making banana fritters every night - I had a good break from these in New Delhi. The sugar was still the same; this contained dead termites or weevils which, when added to your char, floated to the surface and could be skimmed off with a spoon. A new diversion was the local vicar, the Reverend Gordon, inviting bods up for the evening for iced drinks, ice-cream and playing Mah-jong. I enjoyed the cooling intake, but never mastered Mah-jong.

At the technical site, the first of the Listers arrived and I helped Jock Howie make a stand for the trailer it was mounted on, and connect up the electrics. Later two more Listers arrived and we cannibalised an unused Quonsett hut to build a roof over them for protection from the downpours we were now getting. The air temperatures dropped, but the humidity increased, so you didn't really feel any better.

The weeks went by and I was posted to Char Chapli, an island station in the Loran chain. I said goodbye to Archie and Ron and got to Cocanada Port where I joined a seething train bound for Calcutta. An Army Major invited me into his private compartment, bought my meals and helped me dodge the ticket inspectors. At the Howrah station in Calcutta I managed to get on an RAF gharrie to No.228 Group, Barrackpore, several miles out of Calcutta. RAF Air Bookings told me I would have to wait three days for a flight, so I lounged about in Barrackpore and spent the time with some bods I knew back in Sambre.

31st May 1946.   RAF Char Chapli, 20310 AMES

A Beachcraft aircraft, having four or five passenger seats, took me from RAF Dum Dum to Char Chapli, a flight of about one hour. Not knowing what to expect when the kite started to circle around, I was a little apprehensive when the sea and shore line appeared nearly upside-down. I looked down to see where the landing strip was; I couldn't see it, because there wasn't one. We touched down on the beach, the tide being well out. In no time at all a gang of long haired, stripped-down bods rolled up in a jeep and a 15cwt Chevvy with yells of delight, because to them this was the weekly provisions flight, also bringing in mail, fuel oil, cine-films and other necessary stores. I realised that the pilot's antics had been a signal to everyone in the camp to get into the transport and meet us on the beach.

Char Chapli was an island somewhere in the outer mouths of the river Ganges, not to be found on any map. In fact, only a few families lived in half a dozen bashas, more a hamlet than a village. Our domestic site was fairly near to the beach, consisting of Quonsetts, bashas and a duck pond. The hamlet was further inland, and a mile beyond that was a river with a jetty, to which a kisty (small boat) sometimes delivered mouldy bread and livestock. I was delighted to see George Johnstone and I moved in with him. The technical site was over a mile away the only access being via the beach, so we went on watch in the jeep, or in the 15cwt if any diesel oil or other stores had to be taken. The radar equipment was the same as that at Cocanada.

I soon settled down to a routine. Although near to the beach, not many used it because there were said to be alligators lurking in the shallow sea. I had a dip sometimes to cool off when on watch at the technical site - I never saw any alligators. In the evening, our after dinner walk was past the hamlet to the jetty and back. The presence of our camp dogs made the local dogs howl and bristle and we sometimes had to jump to the rescue of our dogs. I had inherited Salty, a very friendly little mongrel bitch, from her previous guardian who had been posted somewhere.

Soon I was asked to repair the ciné projector, which was really worn out, but I got it going again and immediately became the camp cinema operator. The shows were held outside, near the duck pond, and I played records until everybody had brought their own chairs or boxes, the local Indians standing at the back. Once, one of them crept to the back of the screen to see where all the people were coming from! The wireless mechanic had wired up speakers into the Quonsetts, and the locals would point to them and say "Ah, Chota Admi (little man) inside". I don't know how they thought an orchestra could get inside as well, when music was playing.

RAF discipline was virtually non-existent, but one day our CO (a F/O) said we had to tidy things up and that he would have a kit inspection. He must have got wind of a visit by the Air Officer Commanding the Group, an Air Commodore. He turned up eventually, chatted to everyone in an informal way, and left quite happy, or so we assumed, since we heard no more from our CO and everybody went back to the easy life.

CHAR CHAPLI

The kitsy pulling into our jetty at Char Chapli bringing bread from Kepapari, (about 12 miles upriver)

The Beachcraft airplane that took me, provisions and mail to Char Chapli

The first Dakota to land (and take off again)
successfully on the beach

Alan Foster and Paddy pose with the Dakota
on the beach at Char Chapli

Loading the dismantled radar
gear into the Dakota

Two diversions kept us busy: an unexploded bomb and a big snake. The bomb was brought into the camp by the locals, who found it goodness only knows where. The CO hastily ordered it to be taken away, a long way away, and some knowledgeable bod exploded it (probably the cook, who receives mention later). Because we had wild life on the camp (goats, ducks, geese) we also had predators, green pit vipers (bright green and fairly small) which were highly poisonous and to be avoided. But one day a large snake (5-6 ft. long) was found near the cookhouse and no-one recognized the species. The locals were hopping around advising that it would be safer just to drive him back into the jungle. However, all we could do was drive him from one basha or Quonsets to another and he ended up in the wireless communications hut and would not come out. In exasperation, the wireless bod said he must be shot. So a 0.303 rifle was drawn from the armoury hut, and shot he was (probably by the cook). The locals disposed of his body (for dinner I wonder?) (The Government of India has recently stated that each year 20,000 people die from snake bites).

After this episode, the cook noticed there were two ducks missing, then a goose, then a goat. It was thought that this was probably not the work of another large snake, and the cook reckoned it must be a leopard. We couldn't afford to have our livestock depleted like this, because bad weather was preventing provisions flights to Char Chapli, and we had already eaten one goat (goat stews taste of goat the way a goat smells - pretty horrible). So one night the cook organised a leopard hunt (the cook was actually a Warrant Officer Air Gunner who had done all his flying tours of duty and was re-mustered as an AC 2 cook, though still on W/O's pay and retaining his rank). As an air gunner he was a little trigger happy; we heard a shot, he'd released the safety catch on his rifle and leaning on it he blew part of his foot off. This kept Doc (the Medical Orderly) busy, especially as no kites were coming in, due to the weather. One hut was cordoned off as a hospital and he developed gangrene, very ill and no visitors. Doc was very worried, and signals to the mainland were replied with "weather still too bad for flying". It was about 14 days before a kite came; it brought diesel oil, no mail or food, but to Doc's relief it took the cook back to Calcutta. We never heard whether he recovered or not. One of our bods volunteered to be cook, but since we were completely out of sugar, margarine, bread and ships biscuits, and he didn't want to deplete livestock, we survived on corned beef and nothing else.

We then had a signal through from Group that the station was to close. There followed several weeks of dismantling the radar gear, packing it into crates, and bringing it all back to the domestic site. Some items were too big for the 15 cwt Chevvy, but we had a big Dodge 5-tonner that wouldn't go, and this was used effectively as a trailer, pulled along by the 15 cwt. A full inventory had to be made of the contents of every crate and box, because the gear was not being scrapped but re-installed in Burma (so we were told; unlikely I thought). But a S/L came in from Calcutta to check everything; we were pleased, not to see him, but to receive provisions and mail - I got 14 letters.

When rummaging round some old American papers one day, I came across this little rhyme:-

I haven't yet learned to speak Pushtu,
It's one of the things that I musht do,
A long time ago,
I had a chance to do so,
But at the time I just didn't wush to.

During these weeks of great activity my left eye began troubling me, until I could no longer see out of it. Doc gave me eye drops every day and said it was probably due to the glare of the sun off the beach; the sand was especially white in the area of the technical site, and he compared my problem to that of snow blindness. When after weeks there was no improvement, Doc covered my eye completely, to give it a rest. I was put on light duties, which kept me away from the white, unwashed sand. About this time a signal came through promoting me to sergeant. I knew that this was the result of the EVT instructors course last Christmas, but there was no mechanism for putting such things up on orders, or entering it up in my pay book (a misnomer; it recorded rank and vaccinations, but was more like an identity card that you had to carry at all times).

So the matter was promptly forgotten by all and sundry and in any case, EVT was a non-starter on a small isolated camp that was closing down. Furthermore, there was no dherzi-wallah to sew on my stripes! Later, at a pay parade back on the mainland I did notice a big jump in pay, although I was still called an LAC.

The time came for airlifting the crates back to Group in Calcutta, and a successful trial landing on the beach was made by a Dakota. Length wasn't in doubt, the beach extended for miles, but there was some apprehension regarding the ability of tide-washed beach to withstand the weight of a Dakota (to be fully loaded at take-off). But there was no problem, and we loaded crates on to a second Dakota, which took off successfully. On 8th July a third Dakota arrived, was loaded up, the engines revved for take-off, but it didn't move.

The under-carriage wheels had sunk into the sand. All spare bods and local Indians were hurriedly summoned, and a lot of pushing and rocking while the pilot revved was to no avail. Ropes were slung round the wings, which were out of reach on such a big aircraft, but rocking was no use. Spades and steel landing strips were brought up in an attempt to dig ramps in front of the wheels, but the wet sand kept collapsing and rocking the aircraft simply made matters worse. So it was decided to try towing: the 15 cwt Chevvy was roped to one of the under- carriages, the driver revved, the pilot revved, we pushed, but there was no movement. It was then decided that a second Chevvy be brought up. I had never seen this one, as it was kept in a basha, generally considered to be unserviceable because it had no brakes.

Miraculously the old Chevvy started, was backed out of the basha but having no brakes it rolled straight back into the duck pond. Bods were then diverted from the beach to help pull it out of the pond, but it couldn't be done. Back to the beach to get the good Chevvy to pull the old Chevvy out. The dogs looked on with amusement. Frantic signals were sent to Group and by late afternoon a Harvard and an Oxford arrived – each with a with a senior officer. But even senior officers could not stop the tide coming in, so the Dak was quickly unloaded and a final abortive attempt (with the two Chevvies) to take off was made. The sea was now lapping round the Dak and the two officers took off in their respective planes before the sea engulfed them. They took the Dak Captain with them (was this ominous?) leaving the rest of the crew with us. That night, the projector wouldn't work, so there was no film that night.

Next morning, we were told that another Dak would come for the crates that were left but another officer (F/O of lower rank) arrived in the Harvard, saying there wasn't a spare Dak back in Dum Dum. Strangely, he didn't speak to our CO, the Daks crew, or anybody else - so what had he come for?

CHAR CHAPLI

Gharrie with no brakes rolls back into the
duckpond at the domestic site

A tow is required so that the two gharries can
attempt to free the stricken gharrie

Now, before he arrived some bods had decided to "rescue" fittings and accessories from the doomed plane. First, the pilots seat went, then the 8-day clock, then the fuselage internal padding, and so on. What our bods didn't take, the locals did (there had also been some looting up at the technical site while all of us were trying to free the Dak). Next day a sergeant Fitter came in the Harvard to officially remove the Dak's instruments, but since they had already been removed, he and the morose F/O left empty handed. Our own CO had by now, obviously received a rocket, and he gave us eight hours to return all items pilfered; failure to do so would result in searches and arrests. Needless to say, everything useful that our own bods had taken was returned, but less useful instruments that the locals had taken were never recovered.

The Dak crew members were still with us, since bad weather was again delaying relief aircraft, and provisions. So another goat was shot. Cricket and volley ball games on the beach were organised, but I didn't join in, having one eye still covered. The CO decided a guard should be mounted on the Dak, a good example of locking the stable door when the horse had gone. Notwithstanding, another bod and I drew rifles and climbed inside the empty fuselage before the tide came in, and we spent a night in darkness, bobbing up and down with the waves (the front undercarriage was firmly embedded but the tail was free, so with each wave the tail floated up, then down). We were decidedly unsteady on our feet next morning. I spent considerable time wrestling with the Hercules petrol-electric generator at the domestic site. It was American, and had the same shortcomings as the diesel generators had at Cocanada, i.e. batteries losing their charge and the engine racing, producing voltage surges. I put some sheet metal electrodes in a tub of water to act as a governor and minimise the surges. Meanwhile, at the technical site the tower masts were being taken down. The locals did a magnificent job as they could climb barefoot. One had his big-toe nail ripped right off and another was stung by a scorpion, but they never complained.

Arrangements were made to continue the transport of the gear by sea, and an ASRU pinnace arrived. This was an RAF Air Sea Rescue boat, crewed by RAF personnel. It was loaded up, firstly with the tower mast sections, then crates and boxes all around where space could be found. Doc had decided that I should leave with it and get to see the MO in 228 Group, Calcutta. So I took aboard my kit, my dog Salty for whom I had made a leather collar (to show she wasn't a pi dog) and I was joined by a bod called Fred Tunnicliffe, who hailed from Stoke-on-Trent. Salty was no trouble at all, but Fred was one of these accident-prone types. When we got going, he thought he would get a bucket of water to help him cool off, but he did not realise the speed at which we travelling, there being no reference points in sight. He leaned over the side with bucket in hand and was promptly pulled overboard. Neither did he realise that reflection of the sun from the calm water all around could increase its burning power. He didn't wear a shirt and his upper body got badly burnt; he was later admitted to hospital.

We tied up for the night at a place called Barisol, and were wined and dined at the European Club by some ex-patriots; we got back to the pinnace in the early hours next morning. Eventually the sea narrowed down to a broad river and after two days afloat we moored at a jetty in Khulna, a rail terminal town. Doc had arranged for me to go from there by train to Calcutta, which would get me to the MO quicker than by river. The RAF camp at Khulna was staffed by six surly bods who cursed their luck at having to stay at this god-forsaken place, while bods like me were lucky in having to spend only one night there. I had a rail warrant to Calcutta and was only too pleased to catch a train next morning; the locals were definitely hostile and no wonder the six bods at the ASRU camp were cheesed off. Two of these bods came with me, they were going to Calcutta to buy beer; amazingly we travelled first class, a pleasant relief.

5th August 1946.   RAF Barrackpore, No.228 Group HQ, Calcutta
On arrival at Sealdah station, there were no RAF or Army personnel around, so I took a tonga to Barrackpore. Although my pay book still gave my rank as LAC, I decided to book in as a sergeant and was told to find a charpoy for myself underneath the grandstand. Airmen and sergeants were accommodated at the Royal Calcutta Turf Club, which consisted of tents around two concrete grandstands. It was decidedly cooler under the grandstands. The officers lived some-where else, but the sergeant's mess was in an imposing old house in a district called Riverside. This was about 15 minutes walk from the race course. Half way along this route was a big Army camp of the Green Howard's and we were allowed to use their cinema at nights.

Army redcaps (military police) were all over the place, and they were particularly keen to arrest anyone who didn't stand to attention during the National Anthem at the end of a show. I reported sick the day after my arrival but the MO didn't say much; my eye was uncovered and I had to continue with eye-drops three times a day. This kept me busy and I didn't report to any other office. Furthermore, I bumped into Fred Hill and Bill Paling and chatting made the time pass easily. Every evening we took a stroll round the race course before kipping down. I received a letter from George Johnstone saying things were miserable at Char Chapli, and that they had petrol dropped by parachute to keep the generator going at the domestic site.

By mid-August the local papers and wireless were reporting on the riots and civil unrest in Calcutta, with arson and lynch mobs, and by the end of a week 3,000 people had been killed. Curfews were imposed and the drinking of water forbidden. All RAF (and probably Army) personnel were given cholera inoculations, plus the usual ATT and TAB for good measure, and my arm swelled up, as it did for everyone else. I had no desire to venture into Calcutta at this stage.

One day, walking to Riverside for dinner, I saw a crowd round a dog that had just been run over. As I approached I could see it was Salty, lying bleeding. She recognized me and gave her tail a little wag. I was wondering what to do when an RAF gharrie pulled up and the driver got out to see if he could help. A helpful Indian gave directions to a Vet's surgery and the driver took me and Salty there. The Indian vet said there was no hope for her and he gave me a towel to hold round her head while he injected strychnine. Needless to say I was very upset, knowing it was my fault for bringing her from a lonely island to a busy city suburb.

TICKET WARRANT

Bengal & Assam railway ticket warrant from Khulna to Barrackpore

BARRACKPORE

> **BARRACKPORE S. P. C. A.**
> VETERINARY DISPENSARY & HOSPITAL.
>
> No. 63
>
> Barrackpore, 4 - 9 - 1946.
>
> Received with thanks from Sgt. W. J. Jackson.
> Rupees Five only. destruction a bitch
> being the amount of hospital charges for treating
>
> Rs. 5/-
>
> L. P. Saul
> Jnr. Honorary Secretary.
>
> B.S.P.C.A.
> CROWN PRESS, BARRACKPORE.

Salty is put to sleep

CALCUTTA

Chowringhee Square

Firpo's, as well-known in Calcutta as Raffles is in Singapore

The G.P.O. building

Bridge over the river Hooghly

Calcutta tram – hang on!

Calcutta bus, hanging room only

One day a bod came up to me in the mess and told me I was to report to HQ office. He must have had his eye on me for some days, for he knew my name and what I was (or wasn't) doing. I duly appeared before the Group Education Officer and the Unit CO, who asked what I was up to! I explained that my orders were to report sick for eye treatment and wait for the arrival of the CO from Char Chapli, with the remaining radar gear. The two officers were clearly agitated and said it was unacceptable behaviour that I had not properly reported to the EVT section. They hinted that I was in big trouble (but probably accepted that I had only followed orders). They formally cleared me from 20310 AMES Char Chapli and said I was temporarily attached to No.3 Group (U). I don't recall what that was. Playing cards with Fred and Bill that night I heard on the wireless "and now a Glen Miller record for LAC Jim Jackson with best wishes from old pals at RAF Cocanada". The transmission was from Radio SEAC in Trincomalee, Ceylon, and the disc jockey (a term not invented then) was David Jacobs!

I sought out a gharrie to take me to No.3 Group (U) HQ, but when I got there they couldn't find a charpoy for me, so they put me in an officer's room, with furniture and a proper bunk - almost unbelievable. This time I quickly reported to the EVT Officer, but they seemed to have a lot of spare instructors anyway and I wasn't given any particular job. In any case, my eye was no better and I was still having drops in it. George Johnstone, Doc White, Ron Hutton and Alan Foster arrived from Char Chapli and I was very pleased to hear all the news; they told me that the sea had broken up the Dakota and that bits were scattered all over the beach. Also, that the Beachcraft that flew me to Char Chapli had crashed near Dum Dum and had been written off.

We mooched around drinking char, looking for old pals by peering into tents, until one day George said to me "why don't we apply for some leave?" Then some movement; I was posted to No.11 Hill station in Darjeeling as an EVT instructor. So I went around the usual jaunt to all sections with my clearance chithee, but the Medical Section would not sign it as I was still "under treatment" which meant I could not go on a posting. After a few more days of mooching around, we applied for leave (it was about a year ago when I had my last leave in the Nilgiri Hills) and surprisingly, in a very short time we got passes to go to a private address in Darjeeling. I went to the Accounts Section, got some back pay, and with some cash I already had in my pocket, I had Rs 900 (about £68) which would be more than adequate for a fortnights leave as a paying guest. We were going to the home of Mr and Mrs Blair, Mr Blair being a Sergeant in the Bengal Armed Police.

19th September 1946.   Holiday in Darjeeling

George and I left Sealdah station at 7.00pm and slept on the train in a good 2nd class compartment. We had to change trains at Siliguri and had a wash and a good English breakfast at the station; we were the only customers, English or Indian, and got very good service. We then caught the narrow gauge Darjeeling Himalayan Railway train after breakfast, arriving in Darjeeling at 6.00pm. The train climbed from sea level to 6000ft on a track that twisted and turned, almost going back on itself.

On arrival, we were surrounded by the usual mob, begging to take our luggage. Seeing no taxis, tongas or rickshaws, we engaged two, each putting our respective luggage on his head, as is customary. They knew the Bengal Armed Police lines at West Point, and after a long walk (I was getting worried about the necks and spines of these two scrawny bearers) we found the Blair's bungalow. Mr Blair was about 40 and of Irish descent, Mrs Blair said she was 28, and of Greek parentage; they had three young children, the eldest being away at boarding school. They were very friendly and told us all about the locality.

On our first day we roamed around and found the Bagmari Club in a beautiful mountain setting, and had drinks and a meal there. Unfortunately, it was closing down but they said we should use the Gymkhana Club. Later, we found that this was quite nice, but not so posh as the Bagmari. We went with Mrs Blair to No.11 Hill Station at the Jala puhar end of Darjeeling to get ration cards for George and I, so that we could eat with them. Next day we took a taxi to the race course at Lebong, the course being very small because there is not much flat ground available. In fact, at the end of a race the horses went out to a finishing post on the road, the local police closing the road at appropriate intervals. We both lost a bit of money, but we only went as tourists rather than gamblers.

At night we went to the Beechwood Hotel and played housey-housey (now called bingo). I was intrigued to find that they sold Mitchells and Butlers ales (a Wolverhampton brewery) which quite warmed me to the place.

We frequently went to Eve's café, a typically English little tea room, and had a pot of tea with scones, jam and clotted cream. We continued this routine throughout our leave, fitting in many visits to civilian and RAF cinemas. There were periods of heavy rain and misty weather, during which we usually stayed in the bungalow or went to a cinema. On good days the views were spectacular, the snow caps of Mt. Kanchenjunga (28,000 ft) dominating the distant horizon. Mt. Everest could be seen in early sunlight, but we were never up that early. The Bengal Armed Police had rum rations (the nights could be particularly cold) and Sgt. Blair was the key-holder of the rum store. Was it a coincidence that we had many nights of considerable rum consumption? Mrs Blair was furious when one night Mr Blair got into a cot with the children instead of his own bed. I have never really bothered with rum after that holiday.

Who should I bump into one day but Fred Tunnicliffe, he of bucket-of-water fame. His sunburn had healed but his skin was scarred. On another day I bumped into Ron, Doc and Alan from Char Chapli; we had a few drinks and plenty of talking. They were on leave at No.11 Hill station. Some days later I saw Ron and Alan again, and asked where Doc was. They said he had been sent back after being caught in an "out of bounds" area!

DARJEELING

Mt. Kanchengjunga and part of Darjeeling on the hillside

Part of the main street which zig-zags
up and the hillside

Looking down on Darjeeling with
Mt Kanchenjunga towering above

Looking down on Darjeeling with
Mt Kanchenjunga in the background

A view of the Darjeeling Himalayan Railway, the
track doubling round

DARJEELING HOLIDAY

By the Blair's bungalow at West Point

Where did all these rocks come from?

Monika and Mickey with their ayah

Mrs Blair outside the bungalow

DARJEELING HOLIDAY

Puja on the parade ground of the Bengal Armed Police behind the Blair's bungalow

Ron Hutton, Doc, myself and Alan Foster at
no.11 Hill Station, Jalapahar

Bull tied to a stake (on left) waiting to be
beheaded by a single blow

As a final entertainment George and I were invited to attend the local puja, held annually on the BAP parade ground, with the Maharajah as honoured guest. We had previously played snooker with the Maharajah so we went along thinking we might have another chat with him (we couldn't get near him actually). Pujas are holy days, usually accompanied by some sort of ceremony. This one was held in a kind of circus ring and must have had its origins in sacrificing, or spilling blood to appease the gods.

Firstly, large vegetables were paraded round the ring and then with slick swordsmanship they were sliced in half and sprinkled with red powder (to signify blood). The red halves were again paraded round with much noise, chanting and dancing about to pipe music. Then, chickens and fowl were brought in, heads chopped off and paraded around. Next it was geese and next in turn were goats. These were dragged around, all beheaded with a single blow, the ring became quite bloody and the level of excitement increased. The grande finale was the be-heading of a bull. Asian cattle, especially Brahmin breeds, have very thick necks and I wondered what would be the procedure for despatching this large animal with a single blow.

The executioner had an unenvious job, because if he failed, not only would the Maharajah withdraw his financial support for the puja, but also the disappointment of the gods would put a blight on the success of next years harvest. Hence, there was considerable preparation, which involved tying the bull's head to a post at just the right angle to open up the vertebrae in his neck and thus assist the passage of the sword. The bull was then stretched by half a dozen locals pulling on his tail, tug-o-war fashion. A hush descended, then whoosh, his head was off.

The Maharajah signalled his appreciation, the crowd went wild, and all vegetable and animal carcasses were collected together to provide a glorious feast. The celebrations went on all night.

I went up to Jalapuhar to No.11 Hill station to have a word in the EVT office, and a F/Lt Kent told me I should stay there instead of going back to Barrackpore. I explained that I was still attached to No.3 Group (U), but he casually said never mind that, so I moved my kit up to Jalapuhar, said goodbye and thanks to the Blairs (we gave him a couple of bottles of Scotch to make a change from rum) and I waved goodbye to George at the railway station.

11th October 1946.   RAF Jalapuhar, No.11 HS, EVT School

The accommodation here was wooden huts, although there were some bashas. I moved into a double room, the other occupant being a W/O aircrew type, who wasn't at all friendly. This room had a fireplace and although no fuel was provided I could see some ashes in the hearth. It seemed that this bod had been going into a toilet block and taking planks of wood from the cubicle walls for firewood. When all the cubicle doors here closed, the lack of partitioning was not apparent. I was alone in the room one day and the Station Adjutant walked in with an SP wanting to know why I had been burning government property. I denied doing the burning and said it was like that when I arrived (shades of Homer Simpson). They walked off in a huff and I expected big trouble, but I only saw the aircrew bod once again and he didn't say anything, so I never knew what the outcome was. However, I was pleased to bump into Jimmy Dubock, who had been my class instructor at the Northern Poly. I socialised with him, rather than my EVT colleagues who all thought they were gods gifts to education. We did the usual rounds of the Gymkhana Club, Beechwood Hotel, cinemas and so on.

After a few weeks of routine work, preparing and giving lectures, I got an order to return to Barrackpore for official clearance. My stay up at Darj had done me good, my eyesight returning to normal. So I got a travel warrant, had a last meal with Jimmy Dubock at the Chung Hwa restaurant and left next day from Ghum, this station being nearer than the rail-head at Darj. I changed at Siliguri on to the mainline and had to get into a coach that was swimming in water. It took me 42 hours to get to Barrackpore.

21st October 1946. RAF Barrackpore, No.3 Group (U)

After the miserable journey, I booked in with the sole purpose of booking out again, and started the tiresome business of going to all sections for signatures on my clearance chithee. I hitched a lift or two into Calcutta to buy some shirts and a wrist watch costing Rs95 (£14), had some beers at Firpo's in Chowringhee, the fashionable or "downtown" area. Back in Barrackpore I bought a tin-trunk to help me stow all the kit which I had now accumulated, which included a wash basin and stand, a proper camp bed and pukka bedding, plus civilian gear. I booked a gharrie to Sealdah station and was very glad when the train got moving.

The situation in Calcutta was very tense, we didn't really appreciate what was going on over partition of India, although previously coming from Khulna I knew that trains had been stopped by mobs and people from other religions dragged out of the carriages and slaughtered by the track-side. We had to carry Sten guns but we had no ammunition, so they weren't much comfort. I was the only British Serviceman on this, but I got back to Ghum station in twenty seven hours, which wasn't bad.

CALCUTTA

Debris in the street after the August 1946 riots

More post-riot debris

Body of a rickshaw-wallah, lynched during the riots

HOME POSTING

27th October 1946.   RAF Jalapuhar, No.11 HS, EVT School

Back on camp I looked around for Jimmy Dubock but they told me he had been posted back to Blighty, and a lot of other bods too. A letter from George Johnstone was waiting for me saying he'd been posted back, he hoped that I was and that we'd meet up on the boat (I never saw him again). I got a touch of dysentery, but I did not dare to report sick in case I got on the postings list and the MO would not release me. So I just ate lots and lots of bread. At last I saw my name up on orders to proceed to Bombay for transit to England. Again I went through the tedious procedures of getting clearance, including this time, a full set of inoculations and vaccinations. (This is a prerequisite when changing Commands; I was now leaving India Command).

I sent off a lot of personnel effects in my tin trunk, with the address painted on "61 Lichfield Road, Bloxwich, Staffs, UK". These were mainly shoes, shirts and shirt cloth, suit lengths and other gifts and mementos. (The trunk arrived after I was home in Bloxwich - completely empty!). I got a rail warrant and made my way to Ghum station, but there were no trains. The DHR railway men were on strike and in addition, the Ghurkhas stationed nearby were causing bother with ominous demonstrations over something they objected to. So I went back to the billet for another night.

Next day the DHR train was running, but the mainline train from Siliguri was not allowed into Sealdah station, because of the riots. Somehow, from where we were dumped, I got a tonga across Calcutta to Howrah, but neither were there any trains in or out of Howrah. So I got another tonga to a so-called transit camp in the middle of Calcutta which was basically a collection of huts on a large traffic island, fenced round with chicken wire. Other bods who were marooned there advised me to keep my head down, because "volunteers" were being sought to man the armoured car patrols. These were in fact RAF vehicles with RAF roundels and markings; why the RAF was called to do the policing, I do not know (perhaps in other districts the Army was doing it). I kept my head down for a few days, I don't remember where we got any food. I heard that a Military Special Troop train had permission to leave from Howrah, and I managed to get on that. It took two days to get to Bombay, but thankfully a lot of Army bods got off at Najpur, so I was able to stretch out for a kip.

4th November 1946.   RAF Worli, Bombay

I found the huts at Worli seething with bods waiting for a boat home. I grabbed the first unoccupied charpoy I could see, then wandered around trying to find any familiar faces. I bumped into Jimmy Dubock who had been there several weeks since leaving Darjeeling. This did not bode well for a speedy departure. He said Fred Hill and Bill Paling had been there too, but they had been lucky and got on a shipping list. I stocked up on soap, jam, tea and anything I could pack in my kit bags that I thought may still be in short supply in the UK. (Rationing continued, but eased off gradually, for five years after the war ended). After five or six days I saw my name on the shipping lists and said goodbye to Jimmy Dubock who was naturally very glum, since he had been waiting much longer than I had.

11th November 1946.   RMS "Empress of Scotland"

On the dockside at Bombay I had to do some quick thinking, should I line up with sergeants or airmen? The last week at Worli I had been wearing shirts without three stripes and my paybook said LAC, so I went in the airman's queue. We were shepherded along the dockside (not seeing any familiar faces), up the gangplank, and I was ushered right up into the prow of the ship. There were tiers of bunks fixed to the bare steel plates of the hull, which were very hot. The bod below me said he had been in India for six years, because his records had been lost. We cast off, and wandering around I bumped into Jimmy Dubock who was in a different part of the ship! His name had come up on a list following mine, and he had embarked just before we cast off. We stuck together throughout the voyage.

The steel plates of the hull cooled down after we were at sea. My bunk was right up by the anchor port, and a few nights later, before entering the Suez Canal, the ship dropped anchor. The noise of the heavy chain riding over the anchor port casing was horrendous. To be awakened by such a frightening noise caused panic, and about a dozen of us leaped off our bunks and started to run down the aisle. We sheepishly went back to our bunks when we realised what was happening.

We stopped at Port Said in daylight to take on fresh water, and we were soon surrounded by bum boats selling leather goods, carpets, carvings, cotton goods etc. I bought a leather holdall by lowering down some money on a rope, after haggling the price, and hauling it up with the holdall tied on. We were pleased when the ship moved off and the journey to Liverpool was uneventful. We changed into blue uniforms after passing Gibraltar, when the temperature dropped. Disembarkation seemed to take a long time; a few customs men came aboard and eyed us as we were leaving, ignoring the leather goods that most of us were carrying. I don't know where Jimmy Dubock ended up; I never saw him again. I was in a mob directed on to a train bound for RAF Burtonwood (near Preston). We got there about mid-night and everyone kipped down without undressing.

After a day of queuing here and there, I got ration cards, a rail warrant to Walsall, a pass for a fortnights leave and notification of my next posting. That night I arrived in Walsall about 11.00pm with little hope of catching a trolley bus to Bloxwich, but I stood forlornly by the bus stop with two kit bags, full webbing packs and my leather holdall. Who should go past in their car but my cousin Gladys and husband Jimmy. They pulled up and I climbed thankfully into the car. When I rang the bell at no.61, my sister (who was pregnant with Andrew) came dashing downstairs, father shouting to her to be careful. I settled down to a leave that I really don't remember much about, except that later they said I was in a funny mood.

BLIGHTY-BOUND

Jimmy Dummock and I on the Empress of Scotland, about to enter the Suez Canal

Bum boats alongside the Empress of Scotland on the Suez Canal

First view of Port Said, approaching from the
Suez Canal

Warships in the harbour at Port Said

HOME SERVICE

1st January 1947.   RAF Hinton-in-the-Hedges

I arrived at RAF Hinton-in-the-Hedges on a Sunday, one day overdue (I thought there would not be much doing on Saturday), with crumpled uniform and tarnished buttons. The station warrant officer was ex-air crew and had taken to admin duties very seriously. I quickly corrected my off-hand attitude, polished my buttons, and kept out of his way. But I got leave for Christmas, again, strangely, a leave that I don't remember much about.

When I looked in a pre-war Handbook I saw "Hinton-in-the-Hedges population 26". It was probably the same, or smaller, in 1947. It was situated near the Oxfordshire/Northamptonshire border between Banbury and Brackley. The aerodrome had obviously been of considerable size when operational, for there were two or three runways, lengthy perimeter tracks and dozens of parking bays. By the time I arrived these were crammed with RAF vehicles of all types that had been brought back from Europe after the war ended. A good many contained wireless and radar gear, and in the first few weeks I spent most of my time in these, pretending to service the gear with another radar mechanic called Joe Bence. Old lags like us were now re-mustered as Radar Fitters, to distinguish us from newly trained Radar Mechanics who had been on a much shorter course. There were only thirty or forty bods on the station, so discipline was not tight, despite the keen station warrant officer.

The weather was getting colder and despite there being a coke-burning stove in the middle of each hut, this was only lit at evening time and it was perishing cold through the night. We slept with as many blankets as we could scrounge, with greatcoats laid out on top. I rigged up an electric heater with a cast iron cover and kept it on all night under my bed. This was quite illegal and safety wise, a silly thing to do. Thus started the big freeze-up of 1947.

Heavy snow blocked the roads and the provisions lorries traversed fields that had been blown clear by the strong winds. The farmers demanded compensation for the damage done, which upset the CO, so snow-clearing squads were set to work to open up the roads. Orders went up that all personnel should wear their "boots-rubber-knee" (Wellingtons) but I hadn't got any, nor ever had any (remember, they were out of stock when kitted out in Cardington). Furthermore, I only had shoes that were regulation issue in India, but not in England. The CO nearly had a fit when he saw me - but a fit didn't make wellies materialise. I plodded on with wet shoes and socks, dried at night the best I could by my under-bed heater. I don't know whether or not it was a consequence of this, but I was told to report to Paddy the PBX operator and work as a relief operator. I got on well with Paddy, although I shall never forget his voice on the Tannoy for reveille every morning "the toime is now oh-six-turty hours". I didn't mind this job when Paddy was in the exchange, but when I was alone trying to remember who I'd plugged in to who, I found it a bit hairy. I wasn't on it long enough to become experienced.

The months went by and summer came. I had many week-ends at home travelling by train from Banbury to Snow Hill, Birmingham and Midland Red bus. Other week-ends I would visit Brackley or Banbury, pubs, local hops and cinemas. On Sunday mornings, a local civilian who had an MG sports car would arrive to sell a few newspapers (mostly News-of-the-World) although he was actually the civil engineer for the camp. Nearly everybody was friendly with everybody else (until a later influx) and I was quite friendly with Gary, the camp barber. He was very proud of his blond wavy hair; after he cut my hair I would cut his, to his exacting requirements. He said I ought to have been a barber, but he was genuinely in awe of electricians and wireless and radar types. One day he said he'd like to make a crystal set. I said it might be difficult to find the parts, but I found a crystal and some headphones. He asked if he should just connect the 'phones across the crystal I said, an aerial and earth were needed, and a tuned circuit, but it might be difficult to find a suitable coil and condenser for that. A few days later he asked me to come and listen. He'd thrown a bit of wire up into a tree, buried another piece by the tree, connected the 'phones across the crystal, and there it was, the BBC Home Service. I could hardly believe it!

So far I hadn't bothered to sew on my LAC propeller, and one day my name was up on orders as promoted to corporal. So I sewed on two stripes instead. Very soon I was transferred to the guardroom as there was only one proper Service Policeman and a shortage of NCO's as stand-ins. Proper manning of the guardroom was becoming essential, since the MOS (Ministry of Supply) was getting ready for its big auctions of war surplus stock. But I didn't think an SP armband went at all well with my "sparks" badge. Civilians in cars and vans were coming in to view the vehicles and other stock, and it was necessary to check them out, as well as in. The first big sale was just for spare wheels! But wearing an SP's arm badge meant you had to do proper station police duty, such as checking airmen's passes as they went on leave, and their bags - butter, jam and wireless parts were favourite acquisitions.

The camp was now filling up with new recruits, mainly from Eire and the West Indies. They were always giving trouble, and I had to do my stint of taking defaulters parades. If I ordered Jamaicans to scrub the guardroom floor, they would laugh and say "Man, black men don't scrub floors". The Irish boys were always getting into fights or going AWOL (absent without leave). Some went home with their kit and never returned. One did and I had to arrest him, but there was no lock-up at Hinton-in-the-Hedges, so he had to be taken to Group HQ in

Bicester. One day I had eleven bods on defaulters and five more I had to put on a charge. With so many fights in Banbury, the CO thought we should have a police patrol there at nights. Gary liked this idea and volunteered to go on patrol, proudly wearing SP arm-band, white belt and gaiters. I wasn't at all keen on this myself. It was the King's birthday on 5th June and the CO decided to have bags of bull around the camp and a big parade and march past on one of the runways. I'd had enough of chivvying unwilling bods around, hut inspections and so on, so I asked the CO for a transfer to something more technical. I don't know if he remembered the wellies incident, but he put me in charge of the Fire Picket instead!

This was a self-contained little unit, in the middle of the camp near to the runways, an obvious location. It was staffed by five or six young lads (except one, Jock McCristol, who had been a dust-bin man in Glasgow; he never took his socks off, and his feet smelled horrible). The lads told me about duties (there had to be a watch system), fire regulations, routine checks, fire pumps, hoses and so on, and told me just to sit back and take it easy. There was long grass all around where we had to patrol and my hay fever was as bad as I ever remembered it (the last two years, in India, I was not affected at all).

They taught me to drive the fire tender, built on a Commer Karrier chassis, which unfortunately had no floor in the cab and was on its last legs. But they kept it going because it was essential transport to the cookhouse at every meal time. We used to charge down to cook house and jump off the tender yelling like a band of brigands. The lads also made a bicycle for me; they all had their own bikes, made quite illegally from bits and parts from the station scrap heap. (Scrap was still AM property and removing bits was classed as theft). Even so, the CO, who was a Group Captain and ready for release, asked me to scout around and get some good fire buckets "for his own use". I had settled down to a congenial life, and with my bike I was able to get into Brackley every night, to the pubs and for dates. Nevertheless, I caught the CO before he was demobbed and asked him to get me a posting where I could be employed in my Trade. I was posted within a few days to RAF Stafford.

DEMOBILISATION

1st July 1947.   RAF Stafford, No.5 MU

No.5 Maintenance Unit was a very big station (and probably still is) on the outskirts of Stafford. The huts were very large, but even so they were filled with two-tier beds. I thought I'd seen the last of these, but corporals got no preference, and I had to take an upper bunk. Nevertheless, there were several advantages to this camp; the food was very good and I liked the days when we got sauté kidney and fried bread for breakfast; it was near to home, a Midland Red bus ride away; there was a large NAAFI, a facility I'd not seen since Yatesbury days; there was a Corporal's Club which had its own bar and regularly held dances and socials; and there were lots of WAAFs around. I soon made lots of friends of both sexes and it was very relaxing, there being somewhere with a party atmosphere every evening. Even when I went home for the week-end I would get back in time for the Sunday night dance in the Corporal's Club.

Work consisted of repairing, maintaining and re-equipping mobile ground radar. My demob number was 56 but radar trades were being held back; in other trades airmen with demob numbers of 70 and above were being released. So I just sat back and waited, enjoying badminton and table tennis when off duty and the social whirl in the evenings.

Eventually I got papers for the process of demobilisation, and on the 10th October 1947, resplendent in a double-breasted grey pin-stripe suit with shirt, tie and Trilby hat, I caught the Midland Red bus from Stafford back home to Bloxwich.

DE-MOB PAPERS

ROYAL AIR FORCE
CERTIFICATE OF SERVICE AND RELEASE

R.A.F. Form 2520/11

of W. JACKSON (Block Letters)

The above-named airman served in the R.A.F. on full-time service.

from 13.12.43 to 9.10.47.

(Last day of service in unit before leaving for release and release leave).

Particulars of his Service are shown in the margin of this Certificate.

Brief statement of any special aptitudes or qualities or any special type of employment for which recommended:—

A sound N.C.O. of exemplary behaviour who is an efficient Radar Fitter. He is intelligent, studious and well educated. I recommend him for further university training particularly in metallurgy.

Signature of Officer Commanding

WING COMMANDER

Date 8-10-47

SERVICE PARTICULARS

Service Number: 3008723   Rank: CPL

Air Crew Category and/or R.A.F. trade: RADAR FITT.

Air Crew Badges awarded (if any): Nil

Overseas Service: INDIA 1'26" CEYLON 4 MTHS. 21.7.45 – 14.11.46

R.A.F. Character: V.G.

Proficiency A: SUPR
   "   B: (see notes on back of certificate on opposite page)

Decorations, Medals, Clasps, Mention in Despatches, Commendations, etc.

Educational and Vocational Training Courses and Results

DESCRIPTION

Date of Birth: 3.4.24   Height: 5' 8"

Marks and Scars

Specimen Signature of Airman: W. Jackson

Part of the Document of Release, from RAF Stafford. (The Final Curtain? See G Reserve…..)

RESERVE CALL UP

26th July 1952.   "G" Reserve at Portland Bill

By this time I was married to Barbara and living at 41 Oak Hill, Epsom. I was a research metallurgist, having forgotten all about radar. But on the 22nd January 1952 I received a preliminary warning from RAF Record Office, Gloucester, that I was a Class "G" Reservist and "a call-up of Radar and Ground Signalling Trades was required to fill gaps in Control and Reporting organisation in an emergency. A period of 15 days refresher training would be given over dates that could be selected from the list". I duly had a medical examination at Tolworth and was told my dates would be 26th July to 9th August.

On the 17th June, the postman knocked on the door wanting a signature for receipt of a registered envelope; "ere's yer call-up papers" he said. The package contained all sorts of information, including travel warrant, what to take with me, where to report, what to do about income tax and so on.

When I got my uniform I found that my corporal's stripes had been sewn on upside-down, underneath the sparks badge. At the time, technical trade NCO's were identified in this way. I was uncomfortable in my beret, never having worn one before. A further surprise was that in the domestic site; lockers were provided for each airman, there were chairs and sheets for the beds.

The technical site was on a raised area of Portland Bill. The radar gear was completely unfamiliar to me and nobody offered any training. So I did the Times crossword every day, drank tea, chatted and looked out to sea. The end of the first week was approaching; the week-end was a Bank Holiday. "Did I want a 72 hour pass?" I replied in the affirmative, and caught a Southdown bus to Bournemouth and booked in at the Toc

H (remembering happy times at the Toc H in Bath eight years before). I wandered around, spent half a day in Weymouth, the weather was sunny, and my fifteen days training were whittled down to twelve. The second half of my stay at RAF Portland Bill was spent in the same way as the first. I returned to Epsom with my new kit; it is still in the loft in my home to this very day.

G Reserve

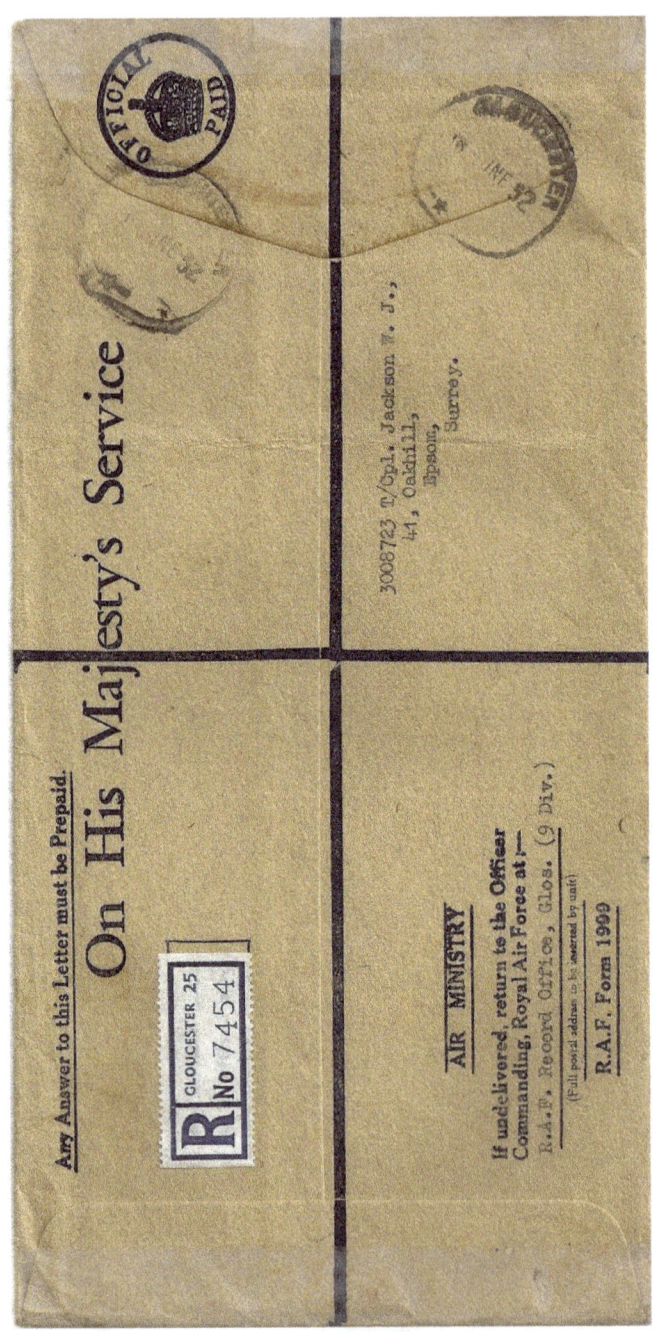

EPILOGUE

I wonder how India has changed in the 54 years since I left. Certainly there will have been many changes in the cities, modernisation and style of living. Judging from various TV programmes of recent times, rural areas have changed very little.

The population is now over one billion. It has tripled in the last 50 years, so that roughly one in six people on earth is now Indian. This statistic means that there are about 72,000 Indians born every day and the number is growing by about 16 million a year. India is only 40 per cent as big as the United States, but has four times as many people.

The only other country in the world where the population exceeds one billion is China. There, this total was passed in 1980 and the present total is currently 1.27 billion. Despite setbacks to progress suffered under the rule of Mao Tse Tung, in the last five years or so major political advances have boosted industrial and commercial progress, whereas in India, perhaps because it is a democracy, religious and political differences have impeded overall growth. India has the biggest film industry in the world, but the output of films is mainly for the home market. The car factories still turn out the Morris Oxford of 35 years ago, although I have read that they will be changing to Austin Montegos! A significant body of opinion is anti-British, but there are those who commend the British constitutional systems that are still retained. India is an enigma, and living there was a unique experience. I was saddened to recently learn that ex-soldiers in the Indian Army (i.e. British) do not receive a pension whereas ex-soldiers from the Indian National Army (i.e. Japanese) still do. The former were faithful and brave men, who suffered heavy losses fighting for the British in Burma, North Africa and Europe.

I wrote hundreds of letters to friends and relations while in the RAF and I still have a record of those I sent in numbered sequence from Ceylon (Sri Lanka) and India. I am sincerely grateful to those who wrote to me, family, relations and friends frequently sending gifts of magazines, newspapers, cigarettes, pipe tobacco and so on. I only wish I could thank the scores of pals and acquaintances for their comradeship and fun, without which life would have been so dull. After demobilisation I kept in contact for a short time with Fred Hill and Jimmy Dubock, with Bill Paling until he died in 1992, and with "Knocker" Alan East with whom I have regular contact.

The Northern Polytechnic is now a University, RAF Yatesbury and RAF Hinton-in-the-Hedges have disappeared under the plough. It all seems so long ago.

APPENDIX

A Few Facts

(NOT a comprehensive review of the 1939-45 war)

1939 3rd September. Britain declared war on Germany because, in spite of our ultimatum, they would not withdraw invasion troops from Poland. Later, with consent of the people involved, Germany took over Austria and Sudetenland (a German speaking region of Czechoslovakia).

1940 10th May. German troops occupy Belgium, Luxembourg and Holland, thereby by-passing the fortified French border which contained the Maginot Line. This preceded the fall of France. Britain sent troops to help France, but were defeated and by the end of May, 30,000 of our troops sat on the beaches of Dunkerque waiting for evacuation.

1940 June. France asked Germany for an armistice. General Pétain (later called a traitor to France) agreed that German troops should occupy northern France, and the southern regions should be under the control of General Pétain, who established a collaborating government at Vichy. Many Frenchmen and French soldiers escaped to England and under the command of General Charles de Gaulle, assisted and fought with the British, as did many Polish, Czechoslovakian and Jewish escapees. But in effect, by the mid-1940s, Britain was alone in the war against Nazi Germany. Adolf Hitler, the German leader, decided to bomb England into submission.

1941 April. German troops invaded and occupied Yugoslavia. As in France, a secret "army" of guerrilla fighters called partisans continued to harass the occupying forces.

1941 Spring. By this time, the bombing had been concentrated on London (called the "blitz" after Hitler's terminology of "blitzkreig"). From autumn 1940 to spring 1941, 40,000 civilians had been killed and two million homes demolished. But Londoners were not broken in spirit and the RAF were effectively shooting down the German bombers over London and the south-east of England. Hitler acknowledged that his attempt to soften up the English prior to an invasion by his storm troops had failed. The bombing raids on London were eased off and he diverted attention to Eastern Europe.

1941 22nd June. Three million German troops started to cross the border into Russia (USSR). Accompanied by 3,000 tanks, they advanced rapidly covering more than 40 miles a day. They took prisoner three million Russians in the first six months of the campaign. The onset of winter slowed down their advance and the Russians were able to stop them. Hitler was prevented from reaching his goal - Moscow, but 600,000 Russian prisoners had died before the end of 1941.

1941 7th December. Squadrons of the Japanese Air Force bombed American warships in Pearl Harbour. Ships were sunk and damaged, and sailors were killed. America, who had been neutral (but helpful to Britain) in the war with Germany, now declared war on Japan. America also joined Britain and declared war on Germany.

1941-1942. Germany had long been obsessed with the "Aryian" purity of their race, which they considered was being tainted by the presence of Jews. They also blamed Jews for the financial collapse of Germany after the First World War. Hitler decided that all Jews in Germany, and in all the German occupied countries, should be expelled, or in the "final solution", exterminated! Jews were herded into concentration camps in Germany and Poland, and in Warsaw a portion of the city was sealed off to contain no-one else but Jews. This enclave was known as the Jewish Ghetto; when extermination gas chambers were ready in the concentration camps, Jews were taken from the Warsaw Ghetto and by summer 1942, 240,000 Jews had been killed. (By autumn 1943 over four million Jews had been killed by the Nazis. By autumn 1944, one million Jews had died in one death camp alone, Auschwitz in Poland).

1942. Italy had joined forces with Germany and called themselves the Axis Powers. Together they occupied the whole of northern Africa (except Egypt), thus creating a threat to the conduct of the war in Europe by Britain and her Allies. The British, under General Montgomery, and supported by Commonwealth, Free-French and American troops, were eventually successful in driving out the Axis forces, after many hard-fought battles in the desert of North Africa. Following on from this, the invasion of Italy began, after Sicily had been quickly taken. There was bitter fighting in Italy, and many Allied troops lost their lives in the battle of Monte Cassino. Resistance was eventually overcome and after Rome was entered, Italy surrendered. But the Germans would not accept this and they fought the Allies on Italian soil. The Italians helped to drive the Germans out of Italy.

1942 11th December. Hitler declared war on USA.

1942-1943. Lord Louis Mountbatten became commander in chief in South East Asia and concentrated on the re-conquest of Burma. The campaign was conducted by General Slim.

1943. After the Italian surrender, the Allies were able to concentrate their war effort in fighting Germany. A policy of bombing Germany into submission did not yield immediate results. The RAF adopted night bombing of German cities and many night raids were carried out; even so, many RAF air crew lost their lives.

1943 25th July. RAF bombers concentrated on Hamburg with devastating results. In effect, Hamburg was burnt to the ground, and

42,000 people killed. Similar attacks were made on Dresden and other German cities, including Cologne. (Fifty years later, the Officer Commanding these bombers, "Bomber" Harris, was criticised in certain circles for the heavy toll of casualties. But the damage done to British cities by heavy German bombing, again with heavy losses of life in London, Coventry and Liverpool and other cities, were equally horrific). Also on the 25th July, Benito Mussolini the Italian leader was arrested by his own Government.

1943-1944. American heavy bombers called "Flying Fortresses" joined in with the bombing of Germany. They could fly at higher altitudes than the British Lancasters and hence daylight raids were feasible. The US Army in Britain began training for the invasion of Germany.

1944 6th June. D-day, the term used to identify the day when American (and other) soldiers stormed the beaches of Normandy in northern France. The operation, under the supreme commander General Dwight Eisenhower and code named 'Overlord', was successful, and one million soldiers took part in the assault. But 2,500 men lost their lives. German troops resisted strongly and the advance through France, Belgium and Holland was slow. Many British paratroopers were killed in the Battle of Arnhem in Holland. Altogether, 36,000 Allied soldiers (the majority American) lost their lives during the advance.

1944 26th August. Paris was liberated and General de Gaulle made a triumphal return to the capital. A second landing of Allied troops was made near Cannes in the south of France. Aided by French Resistance fighters, 9,400 men and 11,000 vehicles advanced inland. French civilian men and women who had collaborated with the Germans were hanged by the resistance fighters. Women in Paris had their hair shaved off and were publicly humiliated.

1945 26th April. Mussolini was shot dead by Italian partisans. Next day, his body was publicly hung by its heels in Milan.

1945 30th April. Hitler committed suicide. He was sheltering in an underground bunker with some German officials, and his mistress Eva Braun. It is believed that he went through a marriage ceremony with Eva, then soon afterwards he shot himself and Eva took poison. In the confusion of the occupation of Berlin by Russian troops, it was not known what became of their bodies. The consensus of opinion of post-war historians appears to be that they were burnt. The bunker itself, over the succeeding years became buried. The Russians are now said to hold the skull of Hitler in the KGB building in Moscow. At the time the Russians entered Berlin, the soldiers had been given three days of permitted looting and vandalism. It was estimated that in Berlin 100,000 rapes were committed and 6,000 German men and women committed suicide. After the occupation, six million German soldiers and three million civilians died as a result of the advances made from the east by the Russians and from the west by Allied forces.

1945 7th May. Germany surrendered and the war in Europe was over. Human misery continued however, for Europe was now full of "displaced persons", i.e. those left homeless, foreign nationals who had been transported into forced labour, and prisoners of war and concentration camps. At a conference in the USSR at Yalta, Churchill and Roosevelt had promised Stalin that all Russian (Soviet) nationals would be returned. Sadly, most of these men and women knew they had no future and strongly resisted repatriation (notably here were Russian Cossack elite soldiers). They were all killed by Stalin whose policy was that everyone who had been in contact with the West, by choice or compulsion, should be exterminated. Britain was later strongly criticised for taking part in sending these people to their deaths. At the end of the war there were 30 million "displaced persons" in Europe.

1945 May - August. The war in the Far East and South East Asia continued. The Japanese had occupied Malaya, Singapore and Burma and thousands of Allied troops (British, Australian and Dutch) were committed to inhuman treatment and imprisonment. (Many thousands of native civilians were similarly mistreated). India remained loyal to Britain, even though the Japanese successfully recruited many Indians into the Japanese army under the name of the "Indian National Army".

The war in the Pacific raged on. The Americans had successfully dislodged the Japanese from some of the islands (including Wake and Iwojima) and on April 1st, the battle for Okinawa began. Expecting to meet with the strongest of Japanese forces, the Americans landed 50,000 troops. However, the resistance was not there, but after the landings, the Americans did not immediately take Okinawa. The Japanese waged a guerrilla war from cave hideouts and attacked with Kamikaze aeroplanes. Two thousand Kamikaze pilots flew to their deaths. American losses were huge, 30 ships were sunk and 5,000 sailors lost their lives. The Japanese had commandeered all the food on the island and civilians were starving. The Japs ordered them to kill each other and handed out grenades for this purpose. At the end of June, the Japanese were defeated in Okinawa; the cost to human life had been high; 150,000 civilians and 66,000 Japanese soldiers and airmen had lost their lives.

The aim of the Japanese in starting the war was world domination; they believed they were the master race, with a divine Emperor, and the armed forces were indoctrinated to uphold this belief, their own lives being of lesser importance. They commenced their territorial occupations with the annexations of Manchuria in north-east China and (later) the peninsula of Korea. Their occupation of Manchuria (which they renamed Manchukuo) was particularly harsh, requisitioning food, using terror and torture and live Chinese for bayonet practice, and generally demeaning the Chinese population. Schools were taught in the Japanese language and slow-learners were hit by Japanese teachers (as indeed were Japanese soldiers by Japanese Officers).

The Chinese were resisting further Japanese expansion, but in 1936 they were also fighting each other. The Government forces (China became a republic under Sun Yat Sen in 1911) were led by General Chiang Kai Shek; their opponents were led by Mao Tse Tung, a peasant who had succumbed to the teachings of Marx and Lenin and was intent on converting the entire nation to Communism. By 1937, the Nationalists and Communists were never fully united against the Japanese and the state of Manchukuo became established with a Chinese puppet emperor. USA had backed the nationalists under Chiang Kai Shek and after the Pearl Harbour bombing, the Americans decided to help defeat the Japs in China. By the end of 1944 American bombers were over Manchukuo and raids continued in 1945 during the Pacific campaigns. Air raids were also taking place over Japan and President Truman (who followed Roosevelt as president of the USA) ordered the Atomic bombing of Hiroshima and Nagasaki on the 6th and 9th August respectively. It was estimated that 140,000 people were killed outright, but many more died from radiation causes in later years.

On 15th August, Emperor Hirohito persuaded the Japanese Government to surrender. He later (January 1st 1946) publicly disclaimed his traditional divinity and adopted a more democratic image. In Manchukuo, Japanese nationals were slaughtered and their property looted. Russian troops entered and looted from both the Japanese and Chinese. The Russians were mainly boys who had not fought the Germans; they were sloppy, undisciplined and poorly dressed and were soon hated by the Chinese people. Mao Tse Tung's communist army took over and expelled them, and also defeated the Nationalist Army (who later evacuated and took over the island of Formosa, now called Taiwan).

1945 2nd September. US General MacArthur received the surrender of Japan aboard the ship USS Missouri. Admiral Lord Mountbatten (later the 1st Earl Mountbatten of Burma) accepted the surrender of 750,000 troops in his area of command, at a formal parade in Singapore.

Post War. For agreeing to use their territory during the war in South East Asia, India was promised independence at the conclusion. During the war, some Indian politicians and factions were sympathetic to Germany and to Japan. Nevertheless when Japan and Germany surrendered the Indians were keen to see Britain's promise upheld and talks began with the British Viceroy, General Wavell. It soon became clear that the Islamic and Hindu peoples wanted separate sovereignty and a plan for separation was hurriedly adopted. North-east and North-west India became the Islamic state of Pakistan, the rest remaining as India (although the region of Kashmir is still un-resolved, and East Pakistan later became Bangladesh, a separate country). The communal and social aspects of partition were not considered in depth and the two-way transport of Islamic and Hindu communities led to much bloodshed. In the resulting confusion, Lord Mountbatten was appointed as Viceroy, becoming the last Viceroy of India and subsequently, the first Governor General of India until 1948, when full independence was established. He took much of the blame for the disastrous events resulting from partition. (He was killed by the IRA when aboard a small boat off the shores of Ireland). India became a democracy and stayed within the British Commonwealth of Nations; Pakistan withdrew but applied to re-join during Margaret Thatcher's period of prime-minister-ship.

Calcutta has now abandoned its colonial past by changing its name back to the original Bengali name of Kolkata. This comes more than three centuries after the East India Company established the city as one of its key trading posts. Similarly, to mark 50 years of independence from

Britain, Bombay has been renamed Mumbai and Madras is now Chennai.

Ministry of Defence Medal Office
Building 250
Imjin Barracks
Innsworth
GLOUCESTER
GL3 1HW
Tel: 0141 224 3600
Email: Medals@SPVA.mod.uk

Our Reference: SPVA/MODMO/HISTORICAL/WWII(RAF)/1594260

Date: 11 December 2008

Dear Mr Jackson

MEDAL ENTITLEMENT – 3008723 WILLIAM JAMES JACKSON

Thank you for your recent letter regarding your medal entitlement for your service in the Royal Air Force during World War Two. We have examined your record of service and can confirm that you qualified for the War Medal 1939-1945. This medal will be dispatched to you shortly.

With regard to your possible entitlement to the Defence Medal it might help if we give you the criteria for this award:

The Defence Medal is awarded for 3 years (1080 days) non-operational service in the United Kingdom between 3 September 1939 and 8 May 1945 or one year's non-operational overseas between 3 September 1939 and 2 September 1945.

Your record shows that you enlisted into the RAF on 13 December 1943 having previously served in the Home Guard from 30 September 1942. You served in the UK until posted to India from 22 January 1945 where you remained until after the end of the war in the Far East on 2 September 1945. Your total non-operational wartime service amounted to 1070 days which is, unfortunately, just too short to qualify for the Defence Medal.

We are sorry to send what must be a disappointing reply.

Yours sincerely

T CHALLIS
MODMO
for Chief Executive

The Under-Secretary of State for Defence (Armed Forces) presents his compliments and by Command of the Defence Council has the honour to transmit the enclosed Awards granted for service during the war of 1939-45

www.ingramcontent.com/pod-product-compliance
Lightning Source LLC
Chambersburg PA
CBHW070619300426
44113CB00010B/1591